MW01228457

PANIC ATTACKS AND ANXIETY RELIEF

AN EASY GUIDE TO FIGHT ANXIETY WITHOUT
DRUG THERAPY, MANAGE FEARS, CONTROLLING
PANIC DISORDERS AND CREATE A RICHER AND
MORE MEANINGFUL LIFE

MARKUS LOST

PANIC ATTACKS AND ANXIETY RELIEF

An Easy Guide To Fight Anxiety Without Drug Therapy, Manage Fears, Controlling Panic Disorders And Create A Richer And More Meaningful Life

Markus Lost

Copyright 2020

ALL RIGHT RESERVED

This document is geared towards providing exact and reliable information in regards to the topic and issue covered. The publication is sold with the idea that the publisher is not required to render accounting, officially permitted, or otherwise, qualified services. If advice is necessary, legal or professional, a practiced individual in the profession should be ordered.

- From a Declaration of Principles which was accepted and approved equally by a Committee of the American Bar Association and a Committee of Publishers and Associations.

In no way is it legal to reproduce, duplicate, or transmit any part of this document in either electronic means or in printed format. Recording of this publication is strictly prohibited and any storage of this document is not allowed unless with written permission from the publisher. All rights reserved.

The information provided herein is stated to be truthful and consistent, in that any liability, in terms of inattention or otherwise, by any usage or abuse of any policies, processes, or directions contained within is the solitary and utter responsibility of the recipient reader. Under no circumstances will any legal responsibility or blame be held against the publisher for any reparation, damages, or monetary loss due to the information herein, either directly or indirectly.

Respective authors own all copyrights not held by the publisher.

The information herein is offered for informational purposes solely, and is universal as so. The presentation of the information is without contract or any type of guarantee assurance.

The trademarks that are used are without any consent, and the publication of the trademark is without permission or backing by the trademark owner. All trademarks and brands within this book are for clarifying purposes only and are the owned by the owners themselves, not affiliated with this document.

INTRODUCTION

Fear can kill you. It sounds a bit harsh, but it's true. I am referring to the metaphorical understanding here because anxiety and stress can prevent you from realizing your full potential. I mean, in the true meaning of the word.

I THINK IT'S A SIGNIFICANT LOSS

Everyone experiences moments in their lives when they are stressed or anxious. Some people can get rid of stress from the horn and strength through everything that happens. Others (including me) have a harder time dealing with anxiety and fear.

Anxiety is a mental health problem, but persistence can cause many symptoms and disorders that are real and very debilitating. They can start as very harmless (such as digestive problems or unexplained skin conditions). If this option is not activated, the problem can worsen and cause disorders such as depression and insomnia.

After a long period of constant anxiety and stress, your body is far more vulnerable to severe, sometimes life-threatening illnesses such as heart disease, high blood pressure, and diabetes. Some people begin to associate this constant pressure with the body with certain types of cancer.

Why would anyone want to spend their lives with all these negative results: depression, anxiety, or anxiety? That is not fair. I want to help.

After experiencing many problems with stress, anxiety, and depression, I can honestly say when people tell me that they have difficulties.

Fear kills my social life because I suffer from agoraphobia, which means I am too afraid to leave home. Fear also had a direct impact on my finances - I couldn't leave the house so that I couldn't work; I lost my job (which complicates my misery)! When I realized that my fear began to overwhelm me physically, I realized that I had to do something. My back is a constant knot, and I can barely move my neck. I'm always tired. Almost every time I leave home, I experience panic attacks, and my stomach continually swells and discomforts whatever I eat. I knew I had to make changes and improve myself before these terrible conditions recovered from myself!

Fortunately, there is a lot of information that is easily accessible. Not all are good, and not all are successful, but some of them succeed. Some of them make a little difference, and others make ALL the difference. Thanks to everything I have learned, I now live my life to the fullest! I have a great job that I like, I have a beautiful woman for myself, and I have more energy than I ever thought possible!

And the good news is that you can too!

There are several ways to deal with anxiety and stress. I have found that some of the most powerful and easiest ways are natural remedies.

I know, sounds a bit like hippie writing this, but I promise you, the strategies in this book can change your life. It changed mine. I am no longer worried about panic attacks. I don't have agoraphobia anymore. I am no longer a hypocrite. I got rid of my fear of heights, and I was more confident than before.

And it only takes a few days to go through the steps that I shared with you in this book.

You might be skeptical. But did you know that at first, I didn't know what I was doing? With this guide, you can download it faster! I wrote this book for people with various challenges. Therefore, I discuss many reasons. Here are some very important things that can help you, and maybe some less critical things.

This book is designed to help you quickly find the best tool for you. This means you don't need to read the cover of the book to discover it. In fact, I hope most people won't! The only thing I can really recommend is that everyone reads the KEY TECHNIQUE because this brings the fastest return (and sometimes the most powerful) to your time.

If this does not completely solve your problem, go directly to the chapters that are best for you. Think of it like a buffet: You choose the things that interest you.

Don't feel guilty if you don't read the whole book. Get value from the work I wrote just for you and get tools to make your life better!

What are things to look forward to in this book?

This book focuses on the struggle related to fear in general. I will cover everything from permissions to add-ons. These tools can be very powerful for dealing with many challenges that people face: depression, general anxiety disorder (GAD), phobias, insomnia, and more.

Even if you are not diagnosed, but you know you feel pressured, the tips and exercises in this book can be very helpful. I will discuss the big challenges in detail in each chapter, but I only know that these techniques and tools can really help everyone live a more productive and stress-free life!

GENERAL ANXIETY DISORDERS

What is a generalized anxiety disorder? GAD can be a long-term illness where you are more concerned with various situations and problems than with certain events.

People with GAD feel anxious almost every day and often have difficulty remembering the last time they felt calm. After the situation they are worrying or thinking about is resolved, other problems can arise. GAD can cause psychological and physical symptoms. This varies from person to person but includes some or more of the following.

- Fright
- Fear
- Feeling "nervous" all the time
- Difficulty concentrating
- Irritability
- Dizziness

- Fatigue
- Heavy, fast or irregular heartbeat (palpitations)
- Muscle aches and tensions
- Trembling or shaking
- Dry mouth
- Too much sweating
- Shortness of breath
- Tummy ache
- Feeling sick
- Migraine
- Pins and also needles
- Trouble sleeping or staying asleep (insomnia)

ANXIETY CAUSES

If you're anxious, it can be as a result of a detail or because of a panic attack, you'll normally recognize the reason. For instance, if you have claustrophobia (concern of confined areas), you know that being constrained in a small area will certainly cause your anxiety.

However, if you experience GAD, you may not always recognize the source of your anxiety. Not knowing the triggers for your anxiety can magnify it, and you might start to fret that there's no solution.

Individuals suffering from GAD might likewise discover that they are extra susceptible to various other anxiety-related issues like hypochondriasis, panic attacks, etc. This is something I experienced though it took a fair amount of time before I identified exactly how to reclaim control of my life.

MY EXPERIENCE

Provided the rather consistent chronic nature of the symptoms, a lot of individuals might not also understand they have GAD. I was certainly in the camp of I feel great. Often I might be a little stressed out, but otherwise, I 'm fine".

The issue was that I wasn't' fine. My body was frequently in the fight-flight setting. This is incredibly fatiguing on both body and mind.

To battle my first signs and symptoms, I started using caffeine to make me wide awake and focused. This was benefitting for only a short time, and after that it stopped producing the desired result. I tried utilizing even more caffeine, yet there's only so much cups of coffee you can consume in a day before you realize that no amount is enough to suffice.

When I chose to surrender caffeine as well as treat myself is when I recognized just how broken I was. Without coffee, I struggled to rise early in the morning, regardless of ensuring I had 8 to ten hours rest. My mind refused to function. I couldn't keep words in mind; I couldn't find out any type of new information or maintain anything. I felt clinically depressed, nervous as well as powerless all of the moment.

While all that sounds like fantastic fun, what has it got to finish with GAD?

Well, I genuinely believe there are hundreds of individuals out there who are dealing with GAD as well as masking it with caffeine, pure nicotine as well as other substances simply to survive the day.

WHAT CAN YOU DO TO CONQUER IT?

GAD is somewhat different than other panic disorders in that it's not a single event that occurs periodically; instead, it's a continuous state. Thus, the approaches used to conquer it need to be made use of on an ongoing basis too. Thankfully, this is easy.

My experience of GAD manifested itself as agoraphobia, hypochondria, and also consequently, an anxiety attack. Yours will probably be something different. Despite the signs, the techniques to conquer it will undoubtedly be the same, as well as the results you can receive from it, will be just as effective!

COHERENT BREATHING

Coherent breathing is merely the practice of reducing your breathing to a piece of 5 breaths per minute. It's as easy as counting to 5 on the inhale as well as counting to 5 on the exhale. You simply repeat this for five minutes. Easy, huh?

This easy and powerful strategy will certainly calm your nerves in a more long term method. What you'll find contrasted to other breathing strategies (like the 4-7-8 breath which I will explain in the next chapter) is that they are really instantaneous as well as noticeable in their impacts. Coherent breathing has the same results, yet it takes place in a slightly different means. You'll discover it still provides that calming impact, yet it is a lot more subtle, so it leads to a longer duration of calmness and helps you to relax. These qualities make it perfect for taking care of GAD as the impacts of the breathing tie in perfectly with the symptoms of the disorder:

As a quick review.

- Breath out with your mouth for the count of 5
- Breathe in via your nose for the count of five
- Repeat for five minutes

This exercise should be carried out two to three times daily for at least a week. If you committedly try it for a week and then decide it's not for you, fine; there are numbers of various other techniques in this book you can try. Yet I have actually seen this simple exercise dissipate concerns like GAD not just for myself but also for others. I truly believe it's worth a shot.

Have you obtained an extra 15 minutes a day to do away with your stress and anxiety? I assumed so. Try!

2

BREATHING

Why is it important to control breathing?

Everyone has to breathe, right? If you don't breathe, you don't do much else. But what is so important about respiratory management? You might think, "So far, I have accomplished a lot in my life, and I can breathe alone!"

That is true. And for many people, they are not interested in learning how to "breathe."

However, you must be VERY interested. In our case, we talked about how breathing can relieve anxiety symptoms and related conditions - it was almost a miracle.

BREATHE ANXIOUSLY

When we feel anxiety, our breathing changes. We begin to take short, shallow (very shallow) sometimes even hyperventilating breaths. This is usually referred to as "excessive breathing."

This book provides techniques for dealing with "breathing." This type of breathing can make you more anxious by increasing your heart rate, dizziness, and the causes of your headaches (not the things you want when you are trying to calm down).

It's amazing how real physical symptoms can be when you talk about thoughts in your head and breathe a little. The result is that you can fix both problems with the same tool. Breathing technique is an extraordinary portable tool that you can use when you feel anxious. However, some require practice (if there isn't much, don't worry).

The reason they work so well is that they quickly and effectively eliminate your body's response to fight or flee. This is almost exclusively the reason for the physical symptoms associated with anxiety.

Panic attacks and GAD are examples when your body is in battle or flight mode for short or long periods of time. In other conditions (such as depression), this may be because the body is in battle or flight mode for so long that it attracts and produces negative thoughts related to all the energy needed to fight so much energy is expended for—a long time. Because we have achieved this through breathing, it can be a very good thing to get out of it.

Stay with me if you want to learn something that can change your life.

TECHNOLOGY

The book contains a lot of information. Let's hope it's at least partially useful. If you are like me, buy a self-help book, read, take notes, and motivate yourself. Then you might only remember one thing in this book.

All right, I'll save your time - that's ONE thing: 4-7-8 breaths.

All the techniques described in this book help someone. Some of them deal specifically with the experience that is happening, such as panic attacks. Some of them are for topical problems such as depression or GAD. But everything is intended to help you regain control of your physiology.

What is the breath 4-7-8?

Breath 4-7-8, developed by Andrew Weil, is referred to as a "natural dot." That sounds like something we need!

This method has some of the same benefits of depression as mediation and helps your body relax immediately. Several quotes from the inventor help explain this technique:

"Regular, conscious breathing can calm and stimulate, and can even help with stress-related health problems ranging from panic attacks to indigestion."

"Because breathing is something we can control and regulate, it is a useful tool for achieving a calm and clear state of mind." "Breathing is the best fear method I have found."

WHY USE IT?

The reason why I emphasize this technique is that it's simple and easy to remember when you panic. This also works really well.

It was the first breathing technique I learned and played a BIG role in my journey to get rid of anxiety and panic attacks.

You can do it in a public place without looking like a crazy person (important if you have a panic attack in a public place and can't get aside).

In this modern world, we can be bombarded with things that make us feel insecure and depressed. This routine can guide our body and mind to get accustomed to living in a state of constant combat flight, which can cause problems in the body, such as:

- Increased stress hormones
- Short breathing
- Panic attacks and anxiety
- Increased blood pressure

These are all-natural and normal responses from our stress response system but are strengthened by our environment. Fortunately, with techniques like 4-7-8 breaths, you can quickly and easily regain control of your physiology.

METHOD

How do you practice this magical technique?

1. Sit comfortably in the back position
2. Place the tip of the tongue directly behind the front teeth in the back of the gum
3. Extend the diaphragm and inhale slowly through the nose up to four counts
4. Hold your breath for another seven counts
5. Open your mouth slightly and throw away eight pieces, narrowing your diaphragm
6. Repeat this cycle four times.

You always want to breathe gently through your nose and exhale loudly through your mouth. The tip of the tongue remains in the same position all the time. Exhaling takes two times longer than breathing.

The total time you spend in each round doesn't matter. 4: 7: 8 counts (pun intended). If you have difficulty holding your breath, speed up the exercise as needed, but maintain a 4: 7: 8 ratio for the last three cycles. After practicing, you can slow it down once you get used to it. Inhale and exhale deeper.

The whole process only takes a few minutes and can end your reaction to fight or flight immediately. It is ideal if you have panic attacks or just need to relax quickly.

Dr. Weil recommends that you practice "relaxed breathing" twice a day for at least six to eight weeks to perfect it. He also said that this technology has become more efficient. He mentioned that people had used this exercise not only for anxiety and stress but also for other things such as reducing cravings.

WHAT CAN YOU EXPECT?

You may feel light for the first time after this exercise. This is completely normal and will pass quickly. Dr. Weil advises not to take more than four breaths at once in the first month of exercise (so follow the instructions of a good doctor).

Although the anti-anxiety-calming effects of this exercise can be tested immediately, the true strength of this technique comes from regular daily exercise. By consciously practicing this deeper rhythm, we create more effective subconscious breathing patterns and thus integrate physiological effects into our daily lives. With enough practice, you should start breathing deeper without thinking about it.

If you use this technique to relax before going to sleep (more often than not), some people will tell you that they don't remember passing the first set 4-7-8 before falling asleep!

This is a simple method that can stop fear in its path very effectively, create calm and inner peace immediately, and eliminate the fight or flight reaction. This slows the body's inflammatory response to all these stress hormones.

Try. Thank you later

3

WHAT IS A PANIC ATTACK?

*P*anic attacks are bullshit. Let me put it there. If you have ever experienced it, you know what I'm talking about.

What's disturbing is that your body is just doing its job. He believes you are in danger, so it starts in battle or flight response.

Google defines panic attacks as:

A sudden feeling of acute and debilitating fear.

In short... uneven.

Some people rarely experience panic attacks, while others sometimes follow it every day. If it's you, I can feel your pain, I can feel your struggle, and I only know that there are many very simple solutions that you can apply today.

When I personally suffered from these seizures, I suffered from extreme agoraphobia and could hardly leave my room. Then I was very worried about driving, especially on the highway, and I would feel an attack if I thought about it if I only thought I had to drive one by one.

There are not always rhymes or reasons for panic attacks. Sometimes, like my highway trip, it's very clear, which will make it difficult. I am very concerned about this particular situation.

I also experienced panic attacks outside the room, for no reason, in situations where I often had no problems.

I have had dinner with a better half family; it was fun.

According to statistics, at least every tenth person has a panic attack at the same time. Likewise, at least one in 50 people have panic disorder.

In the United States alone, more than 60 million people suffer from panic attacks, and more than 3 million people suffer from panic disorder - this means panic attacks and panic disorders are not uncommon! So don't worry, you are not alone!

Signs and symptoms of panic attacks

The signs and symptoms of panic attacks tend to appear strongly. They usually peak in a few minutes and can take up to 30 minutes (usually much less!) And sometimes come in waves.

People with panic attacks usually find that they have one or more of the following diseases:

• Suffocation

- Sweating
- Stomach ache
- Dizziness
- Hyperventilation
- Dry mouth
- Chest pain
- Hot and cold bursts of feeling suffocated
- Fear of losing common sense
- Fear of death

If you experience a panic attack and you see one physical symptom, you might be mistaken to believe that you are suffering from a physical disorder based on the actual symptoms that you are experiencing. Not so. Seriously. Have you ever had a panic attack, and you are OK? Without a heart attack, you are still healthy, have no ongoing health problems, etc. In the same way, there is a good chance that you really are not, even if you think you will really die.

Symptoms of panic attacks appear because you have super movements of nerve impulses coming from your brain to other parts of the body. So if you experience panic attacks, your body can release more hormones, including adrenaline. This encourages a fight or run response.

Fighting or flight reactions are anchored in your system. It began with our Paleolithic ancestors when they had to face danger before them or run away to stay safe and alive. Currently, we are still experiencing a fight or flight reaction when we are faced with a dangerous situation or at least a situation that we consider dangerous.

What you might find is that your body may have the same reaction when you experience a panic attack. You can breathe hard or breathe hard. You secrete a lot of carbon dioxide, which makes your blood acidic. This causes more symptoms such as cramps, confusion, and sometimes seizures (very rare!).

This imbalance is not dangerous at all, because once you have calmed down, the body will naturally balance everything. In fact, it's only about breathing more slowly.

If you recognize yourself in everything you just read, don't worry! There are some amazing tools and techniques to overcome this and regain control of your life today!

REASONS FOR PANIC ATTACKS

Experts have not identified the exact cause of panic attacks, but have found that genetics and family history have something to do with it. Those whose family members experience panic disorder also experience it more often.

In addition, panic attacks can be triggered by stress, e.g., For example, talking in public or crossing a bridge, and even some food and drinks can have an impact, as we will discuss later.

OVERCOME PANIC ATTACKS AND PANIC DISORDERS

Now everything sounds rather difficult and dark, but don't be afraid! There are some extraordinary tools and techniques to overcome this problem. Many that you find will have an immediate impact, while others will help you to be more relaxed and happier all the time.

Let's get started

BODY AND GRADE

Step 1 - Practice Meditation Carefully

Meditation is one of the most effective and most recommended natural treatments for panic disorder. This technique is about making you aware of your present moment without making a judgment.

With this technique, you can learn to see things more clearly and focus more on your current situation. According to a study by researchers from the University of Lund in Sweden, mindfulness is as effective as cognitive behavioral therapy in which negative thought patterns are replaced by positive ones.

In another study at Boston University, researchers found that attention helps people with depression and anxiety to release negative thoughts and are no longer obsessed. At the end of the study, participants can get out of their cycle of depression or anxiety.

In addition, researchers have found that meditation can help you sleep better, regulate mood levels, and reduce stress so you can relax and prevent panic attacks. If you want to improve the quality of your life, there is no doubt that mindfulness meditation can really help and is the fun part;

It's fun to learn!

Why meditate carefully?

Getting attention sounds rather roomy and is extraordinary. Yes, Of course, he presents pictures of hippies or monks sitting on the mountain and gently muttering "oooommmmm" to themselves. Even though this isn't the type of mediation we're talking about here, they look like very cool people, right? Maybe they have something to do with all meditation.

What we are talking about is an amazing tool that you can touch so far. However, this helps you recognize symptoms and see them objectively.

Why is this so important? If you have experienced panic attacks, you might be able to testify that whatever starts when you are in the middle, you only think of the worst and most objective situations.

I have a heart attack; I will die. My God, my family, will be sad. What have I done with my life?

What you practice is the ability to step back from the moment, to see objectively and tell the symptoms;

Ahhh, I can see there is a mild feeling in my chest. That's good. That doesn't mean I have a heart attack. Whatever, so.

I understand that there are all thoughts of how I can feel crazy. That's good. There's no need to understand this thought, I just have to realize what that is.

When I look at all of these symptoms, I see that this is really my body's reaction to something. My body reacts too much because I think I'm in danger. But I don't. I will watch these symptoms until they do. Days and days. I continue.

How to practice meditation

The short answer is: keep yourself busy, watch your breath, and when your attention decreases, bring your attention back to your breath.

For a little deeper: find a good seat with your back straight and relaxed on a chair or pillow. You can use blankets and pillows, though a good pillow will last a lifetime. You can sit in a chair with your feet on the floor, free with your legs crossed, in the lotus position (if flexible), knees, and more. However, you are fine as long as you feel comfortable. Make sure you are stable and upright. If your body control prevents you from sitting up straight, you will only find a comfortable position for a short stay.

After sitting comfortably, begin to feel your breath as you enter and exit. Really try to trace the breath through your mouth to your lungs, fill your stomach and then come out. Your attention will surely inhale and wander elsewhere. That happens to everyone. This is really part of the exercise, so don't try it wrong! If you pay attention to this, time, i.e., a few seconds, a minute or five minutes, simply point your attention back to your breath. Don't worry about judging yourself or thinking about the contents of your mind.

You concentrate. Your mind wanders. You pay attention to this and direct your breathing and repeat. This is the practice. This is very easy, but not always easy. Keep ongoing, and you will get results. It's not as easy as I say, "I order myself to stop thinking about everything except the breath I want to focus on. Because you are thinking about cat food or whatever. The point is that you realize that you have strayed from the course. Then you can gently attract your attention to return to breathing and return.

Practice dropping things that you cannot control. Often people become anxious and panic just because they are still worried that certain things will or will not happen. For example; you can't control accidents, natural disasters, other people's feelings, and many other things. Remember that you are not God (unless you feel comfortable meeting God), you are a human being. You cannot control everything you want. So if you have an accident or if your loved one dies, there is nothing you can do but accept the facts and move on. Always try to see the positive side of the incident, however difficult it is at the moment. Suppose you are divorced. Instead of seeing it as a big loss, you can see it as an opportunity to start over. If you begin to see and focus on the positive aspects of everything, you will find more than that. Of course, if you have more good and positive things in your life, is there no reason to make you happier with less fear?

Your blood pressure will also be normal. Stress and anxiety often cause an increase in blood pressure. To restore it back to normal, you must let your blood vessels expand. You can help by taking a deep breath and releasing tension.

Interestingly, fear affects not only your mind but also your body. This can actually cause a lot of physical changes and symptoms. Excessive anxiety can trigger your system's resistance or flight response and cause the lymphatic nervous system to release the stress hormone cortisol. This, in turn, can increase your blood sugar and triglyceride levels.

It can also cause shortness of breath, dizziness, dry mouth, nausea, sweating, and panic attacks.

The really positive thing is that after reviewing your anxiety using these steps, you might find that some potentially long-term health problems can be overcome or at least reduced. When you practice relaxation techniques, you trigger your relaxation response, which is characterized by warm feelings and calm psychic alertness.

Step 2 - Practice scanning the body

Body scan meditation is a popular stress relief practice. If you have panic disorders or anxiety, practicing this technique can really help prevent panic attacks and reduce background anxiety. In fact, this is very similar to progressive muscle relaxation, except that it is about focusing on sensations of body parts rather than relaxing and stretching your muscles.

How to practice body scan meditation

Body scan meditation is similar to mindfulness meditation, which we have just discussed in practice and its application. You are doing something that translates you into the present.

The following is a good and comprehensive implementation of the steps for the big, smart ones:

1. Sit in a chair to breathe or rest, feel comfortable, lying on your back on a bed or carpet on the floor or on your bed. Choose a place where you feel warm and restless. Let your eyes close slightly.

2. Take a moment to connect with your breathing movements and sensations when you are done. Bring your awareness to the physical sensations in your body, especially the sensation of touch or pressure when your body comes in contact with a chair or bed. Release each breath and sink a little deeper into your chair or bed.

3. Remember the purpose of this practice. The

goal is not to feel different, calm, or relaxed; this may or may not happen. Instead, the purpose of this exercise is to increase awareness of the sensations you experience as much as possible by focusing your attention on each part of your body.

4. Now bring your awareness of physical sensations into a weaker stomach and start changing the pattern of sensations in the abdominal wall as you inhale and exhale. Take a few minutes to feel inhalation and breathing.

5. After you are connected with the sensation in your stomach, bring the focus or "spotlight" of your awareness on your left foot to your left foot and to the tip of your left foot. Focus on each of your fingers on your left foot, which arouses a little curiosity to explore the quality of the sensations you find, and you may notice feelings of contact between your toes, sensations of tingling, warmth, or no particular feeling.

6. When you are ready, breathe, feel or imagine breathing in your lungs and then into your stomach, left leg, and to the tip of your left foot. Then, when you exhale, feel or imagine breathing back from foot to foot, through the stomach, chest, and nose. Do this best for a few moments, inhale and inhale again. It might be difficult to commit to him. Practice

this "inhalation" as best you can by approaching playfulness.

7. When you are ready to exhale, release your toe awareness and bring your awareness to the sensation of the lower-left foot - bring gentle investigative awareness to the sole of the foot, rise, heel (i.e., The sensation of sensation that the heel is in contact with the bed or bed). Experiment with the feeling of "breathing with" - pay attention to background breathing as you focus on the sensation of the lower leg.

8. Now let awareness develop in the rest of the foot - up to the ankle, the top of the foot, and directly to the bones and joints. Then, when you breathe a little deeper, point it down all over your left leg. When you breathe, you can lower your left leg completely so that the focus of consciousness can shift to the lower left leg - again, the calf. Shin, knee, etc.

9. Continue to bring attention and mild curiosity to physical sensations in every part of the body - again, the upper left leg, right finger, right foot, right foot, pelvic area, back, abdomen, etc. Breasts, fingers, hands, arms, shoulders, neck, head, and face. Bring the same level of awareness and gentle curiosity to the sensations of the body in every area as much as possible. If you leave each main area, inhale and release it from this fire area.

10. When you become aware of tension or other intense sensations in your body, you can "breathe it in" - by gently breathing it to make the sensation sensitive and, as good as possible, develop a fire for it. Or release.

11. The mind will avoid breathing and from time to time. That is very normal. That's what the mind does. If you realize it, admit it carefully, pay attention to where the mind goes, and then focus your attention on the part of the body that you want to focus on.

After "scanning" the whole body in this way, take a few minutes and notice the whole body feeling and free-flowing breath inside and outside the body.

When you fall asleep, it is helpful to support your head with a pillow, open your eyes, or practice sitting rather than lying down.

You can adjust the time spent in this exercise by using larger body parts to become aware or by spending shorter or longer periods with each part.

Step 3 – Emotional Exercises

Not always easy to control nerves. You need enough skills. Just imagine. You are asked to speak. You always dream about that. You know that if you do well, you might be able to get a raise and buy the nice house you've always wanted... but you have butterfly roots in your stomach.

What can you do? What if you could press the magic button that immediately gives you peace of mind and confidence? You know what...

What is anchoring?

In NLP (Neurolinguistic Programming), attachment refers to the process of linking emotional responses to triggers so that responses change quickly and strongly. In our case, this means that you can use anchors to connect calm mental states with simple internal triggers that can help calm and relieve anxiety quickly.

You do this by attaching a mental state so you can shoot the anchor and immediately determine the state.

SHORT STORY

The appendix is something like Pavlov's experiments with dogs. Pavlov rang the bell when he was fed. Animals salivate when they see food. After this has been done several times, the bell and food are shown together, the bell itself lets the dog salivate. Bad dog.

Anchors are stimuli that evoke states of mind - thoughts and emotions. For example, touching the stylus on your left hand can become an anchor. Some anchors are accidental. So the aroma of bread can bring you back to your childhood. Melody can remind you of loved ones. Touching can restore memory and past conditions. This marker works automatically, and you might not know the trigger.

An anchor means to produce a stimulus (anchor)

when the desired condition is experienced so that the desired condition is equated with the anchor.

Anchors can be visual, acoustic, or kinesthetic and can be installed quickly and easily (only as part of the software).

Installation of anchors

This is a fairly simple process, and once it's done, you can use the anchor whenever you need to rest.

1. Determine the conditions that you want to anchor. For example, calm and relax.
2. Select the anchor (or anchor) that you want to trigger the desired status.
3. Remember the memory or imagine a situation where you could experience the situation. So think back or imagine when you are really calm and calm. Afternoon lazy at the beach or relaxing with friends watching TV, for example.
4. Activate the anchor when the experience is bright and in the desired conditions.
5. Remove the anchor when the experience begins to fade. If you anchor further, if the experience fades, you will anchor a drop of rest and relaxation!
6. Do something else - open your eyes ... count 10 to break the condition and get distracted.
7. Repeat this step several times each time.

Clearer memory. This is not really necessary if the anchor is at the top of the experiment. However, you can strengthen the anchor by gluing it over some experiences like that.

8. Install the anchor and check that it is in the necessary conditions.

9. Stay up to date on situations where you want to experience the desired circumstances. Turn on the anchor to see if there are enough resources.

10. Check the anchor the next day to make sure it is a permanent anchor.

Tips for Anchors

Anchors must be activated in such a way that each time you combine them with imaginative experiences they are effective.

Anchor in experiments containing imaginative conditions.

If you don't have foot disease in the future and are very afraid, stop using anchors. (You will correct negative circumstances!)

There is the knowledge that causes anchors to work that was created by the subconscious.

You can strengthen the anchor by repeating the above process for several days.

If you are in a situation where you really have the condition you want, you can restore the anchor in that situation.

The brace can be a very powerful tool for dealing with anxiety now. It's also very useful for other countries that you want on request.

Do you want to feel excited? Make an anchor.

Do you want to feel more love? Make an anchor.

There are almost unlimited possibilities, but for the purpose of this book, do it that makes you feel comfortable. If you have a panic attack and are waiting for a calm anchor, you will immediately be brought to peace, and that's what we want, right?

DIET

What you eat affects your brain

You are what you eat

We've all heard of it. Usually, this is a well-meaning comment from someone trying to distract you from French fries and burgers for something greener and healthier. I refused to do it, especially when I was young. I think I can eat whatever I want (usually a big bowl of pasta) and I can be fine. And it was like ... for a while.

At the end of my teens, I lost my job. At that time, that was the best thing that ever happened to me.

"So you say I can sleep if I want, sleep 13 hours, wake up if I want, and usually spend my days in the cold and not cold ... Registering sounds great!" That is almost an attitude. Many things have changed since then, and I am not the same person as me. I get better every day and work for big goals, but at that moment, this lazy mindset makes sense to me.

The point is when I get into a routine of sleeping a lot, waking up, eating a big bowl of pasta and cheese (like poppy seeds and cheese for our American friends, only without a beautifully baked blanket), and then I feel tired, categorized and not inspired to the rest of the day.

I sleep 12-13 hours a day and am still tired all the time. What is this about?

Not surprisingly, this "wasted life" happened when anxiety and depression came to visit me. Accidental? I think not. I found a sudden change in energy, and my fear came when I did it get a job and start eating better at work. My fear is gone. My depression is gone. I am happier because I am healthier.

As you can guess from the title of this chapter, my opinion is quite important: **whatever you eat, take your lot!**

There is so much research on how intestinal bacteria affect your mood, and there is so much research on how different foods affect your feelings.

As a simple example: have you ever had lunch? I thought to myself. Have you ever had a BIG lunch? I'm talking a few sandwiches, maybe pasta, carbonated drinks, and chocolate, or donuts to end it?

Now tell me how you feel about an hour after that?

Do you feel asleep and can't think as clearly as before? Do you feel a little slow and slow for the rest of the day? Most likely. If not, you are a kind of medical anomaly and can make a lot of money selling your body to science.

This is just a very simple example of how food can directly affect your mind and physiology.

So it's not too stressful if this additional dose of sugar at lunch can dramatically affect you so that the suboptimal diet can contribute to other things in the long run, namely anxiety and panic attacks.

We already know that excess carbohydrates cause obesity (don't worry, this won't be a diet book). With increasing obesity worldwide, we have seen a strong association with an increase in neurodegenerative diseases such as Alzheimer's, which many scientists call type 3 diabetes because of insulin resistance in the brain. Science then says that excess carbohydrates in large quantities can damage your mind and body for years. The good news is; You can always do something about it.

The answer seems to be to eat less carbohydrates and a higher, healthy fat diet.

Why do you ask?

We gradually see strong evidence of healthy fats that improve cognitive function in Alzheimer's patients.

If this sentence alone does not excite you, the same concept applies to other fields of medicine, and there are many scientists who are truly worried that a low-carbohydrate (ketogenic) diet seems to have a profound effect on inflammation in the body and many other things.

I tried eating ketogenic for 30 days. And I have n0 panic attacks. I started eating carbohydrates again, and they came back.

I also experimented with eliminating caffeine (well, coffee, I'm English, so I definitely don't drink tea), and I got quite deep results. No more caffeine = no more fear (at least for me).

Now I don't want this chapter to be a low carb lifestyle. You will find endless books and blogs that call it the best since sliced bread (intended). What I want to show you is that what you eat can really affect your feelings and preparation.

So when I say; try to avoid caffeine for 30 days and watch your anxiety subside…

I know this works, and this chapter is about showing you this. What you put in your body also has a strong impact on your fears and panic reactions.

So eat better and feel better!

THE NEXT STEP

Quick start guide
So all this is good and beautiful. But how do you do it?

Well, let's keep it simple.

1. Try the 4/7/8 breathing method if you feel

panic attacks, and every time you just want to relax ... try now ... continue, I will wait.

2. Stop caffeine (in only 30 days) - You can go back to double crap, delayed three times after a month if you think nothing has changed

3. Begin daily mindfulness meditation - only 10 minutes. If you have to spend 10 minutes a day on something and this gets rid of your anxiety and panic attacks, are you going to do it? That is what I think.

The idea of one of the techniques in this book is to practice it when you don't need it so that you can easily call it when you need it.

Most of them can be done anywhere, anytime, without anyone paying attention. Even if you apologize for a minute or two and have to go through several deep breathing cycles in the toilet, this is not as comfortable as a panic attack on your desk!

So if you practice, you will find that your fear continues to diminish until you really can live your life to the fullest! You always have a choice, and the choice to eliminate anxiety seems reasonable enough.

CHALLENGES FOR GIVING HEALTH

What makes it so difficult for many people to follow this guide, given the significant benefits of eating healthy?

Most of the problems are just inconveniences. Time pressure makes it easy to get convenient food items such as frozen waffles and snacks from a vending machine. If you are rushing through a station and need something while traveling, there are many quick, easy, and unhealthy choices. At home, it's the same: To eat well, you have to plan ahead, e.g., B. Choose a recipe, make a grocery list, go to the grocery store, and learn how to cook when you do not know-how. Conversely, highly processed options are often as simple as opening a bag.

Practical food also tends to provide three kicks of fat, sugar, and salt, which is a very effective combination. We face a difficult struggle if we intend to eat for health reasons and end up eating foods that are mostly brown in color and contain ingredients that we cannot recognize and that we cannot say. If you commit to eating better, plan to reach that goal.

Move your body

Like a healthy diet, constant exercise is an integral part of all aspects of health. The benefits of exercise for physical health are no secret. Research studies show that exercise also has a positive effect on mental illnesses such as anxiety, depression, eating disorders, and substance disorders, as well as on chronic pain and neurodegenerative diseases such as Alzheimer's. The effects of exercise have been widely studied in depression, where the benefits are usually quite large. Both aerobics (e.g., running) and anaerobes (e.g., lifting weight) can improve mental health.

HOW DO YOU HELP TRAINING?

There are many ways that exercise can be beneficial. This includes:

- Better sleep with improved mental health
- Releasing endorphins, the body's natural chemical for "feeling good."
- Experience success through sports and fitness improvement
- Interference from unhealthy thinking like the Romans
- Increased blood flow to the brain
- Improve management functions such as organization and focus
- Social contact with other people who play sports
- Spending time outside the home (if any); for information about staying out, see the "Shopping Deadline" section.

HOW TO START

When you are ready to take advantage of the many benefits of exercise, follow the steps discussed earlier for activation of behavior. First, determine what is important to you during physical activity. For example, is that something you like or a feeling of caring for yourself?

Find activities that you like, and that might not even be included in the practice label. For example, walking friends, playing tennis, or attending dance classes. The more you enjoy the movement, the more motivated you are to do it consistently.

Schedule a specific training time and schedule it on your calendar. Start gradually so that you don't feel overwhelmed by your goals.

With careful planning, you can add regular exercise to your routine and enjoy the overall positive effect on your well-being.

Overcoming stress

Whatever creates our search for physical, mental, or emotional resources leads to a number of stresses, which make stress an inevitable part of life. As with our emotions, the goal is not to relieve the stresses of our lives, but to learn how to deal with them effectively. In his seminar paper, Hungarian endocrinologist Hans Celie points out that there is a general reaction to stress, regardless of the source of the stress. It doesn't matter whether we are chased or talked about by crocodiles - the sympathetic nervous system will be involved to help us overcome challenges.

At a very simple level, you can think that depression manifests when your cortex thinks negatively abstract and manages to convince the whole brain that it is as real as physical stress.

Robert Sapolski, Why Don't Zebras Get Ulcers

CELIE FOUND that we deal with short-term stress very well: our bodies react, we deal with situations, and our parasympathetic nervous system takes us back to the initial level. However, when stress continues and continues, our body and brain wear out.

The cumulative effects of long-term stress include impaired immune function, digestive and cardiac problems, and mental illness. Aside from the long-term effects of chronic stress, living in a state of being constantly alert is not at all pleasant.

The first step in stress management is awareness. Start by being curious about how you react to stress so that the mind can open up to what you are experiencing. As an example:

- Are you clenching your jaw?
- Is your stomach tense?
- Can you hold neck and shoulder tension?
- What is the quality of your breath?
- What do you think?

With a little practice, we can sharpen our awareness of how stress is felt in our body and mind so that we

can begin to reduce it. Practicing mindfulness can help
in this regard.

**Effective ways to deal with stress in our
lives are:**

- Minimizing unnecessary stress (e.g., avoiding
  people who produce stress)
- Say no to commitments when we have
  too much
- Relax hard and unrealistic standards for
  myself (for example, I have to end this
  project today)
- Focus on what's happening
- Breathe slowly
- Practicing meditation
- Take a yoga class
- The first regular practice
- Progressive muscle relaxation
- Take short breaks throughout the day
- Vacation
- Weather protection outside of work every
  day and on weekends
- Challenge useless thoughts about what to do
- Take time for relaxing activities that you
  enjoy reading or taking a hot bath

PROGRESSIVE MUSCLE RELAXATION

Follow these steps to achieve a state of deep relaxation.

1. Find a quiet place where you will not be disturbed. Silence your cellphone.
2. Sit in a chair with your legs straight and your heels on the floor. Make the adjustments needed to make it comfortable for you. Keep your eyes closed.
3. Switch firmly and then relax the main muscle groups in your body, starting with the feet and moving up. Create moderate muscle tension in every area of the body in seconds. Then release the tension at once and notice the difference when you move. Relax for 30 to 60 seconds before tightening your next muscle group.

The sequence can include:

Lower leg: Pull one foot on your toes to create tension along your hips.

Hips: Bend one leg at a time, bend your legs and stretch your quadriceps in the front of your thighs.

Buttocks: Tense your butt muscles.

Belly: Tense your abdominal muscles and pull your belly button towards your spine.

Breathe: Take a deep breath so your chest can expand and hold. Release the tension when you exhale.

Upper arm: One arm, stretch the muscles in each upper arm.

Arms and arms: Make a fist with one hand in one hand and pull your arms back to your elbows, creating tension in your arms, wrists, and arms.

Neck and upper back: Bend your shoulders to your ears.

Face and scalp: Raise your eyebrows while closing your eyes (you may need to remove contact lenses for this).

———

BREATHE IN SLOW, pleasant breath as you release the remaining muscle tension and place your entire body in a deep state of relaxation. Concentrate on your breath. Follow the sensation of inhaling and exhaling. Every time you exhale, mentally say one word that you associate with relaxation (e.g., "Peace," "rest," "breathing," etc.). Say this word every time you exhale for three to five minutes.

Slowly bring your awareness back to where you are. Shake your fingers and toes. When finished, open your eyes. Watch how you feel.

Practice this sequence at least once a day (ideally twice).

You can shorten the exercise over time if you can release tension better. For example, you can do both legs or both hands at the same time, and only muscle groups tend to strain you.

By combining deep relaxation with words and exhaling, you train your mind and body to enter into a state of relaxation. When you start feeling stressed and stressed, you can take calming breaths, say your words as you exhale, and feel the benefits of all your progressive muscle relaxation exercises.

In a world where permanent work is a bonus, we may feel that we are not able to take the time to rest. However, this time is never lost and should not be considered a luxury item. If you invest in your own welfare, you will be more productive and pleasant.

4

STRESS AND ANXIETY ATTACKS &
PANIC ATTACKS

*I*t's believed that over four million Americans suffer from an anxiety attack, according to the National Institutes of Mental Health. That has to do with 5 percent of the grown-up populace. A lot of scientists feel that number is a reduced quote, as so many people who experience panic or stress and anxiety attack never ever get the correct medical diagnosis and also just try to accept their fate, in spite of the incapacitating concerns that it brings.

UNDERSTANDING THE DIFFERENCE BETWEEN PANIC ATTACKS AND ANXIETY ATTACKS

Initially, I want to be clear that there is a difference; anxiety and panic are not the same thing. They are really carefully associated; however, they are not the same. A lot of the signs associated with both are comparable; which explains the reason why they are often grouped with each other.

Panic attacks are really genuine, extremely horrible, and can psychologically drain people. Lots of people that experience their first panic attack find themselves in an emergency clinic or a doctor's office, anticipating to listen to the most awful news concerning their health.

A lot of the signs and symptoms of a panic attack can lead individuals to really feel as if they have cardiovascular disease as a tight upper body, and heart palpitations are common results of a panic attack. Some people could really feel the concern that they'll "lose control" of themselves as well as can do something embarrassing in front of other individuals.

Panic attacks are generally considered to be abrupt and also exceptionally intense. They do not constantly have a factor for occurring as well as tend to last no greater than 10-30 minutes. Occasionally, strikes can occur in succession so they can give the feeling of a continual state of panic.

After an attack has actually occurred, the person has a tendency to feel worried and on-edge regarding the potential of an additional strike.

Unfortunately, many people do not look for help for panic attacks and associated problems like agoraphobia. This is particularly heart splitting due to the fact that panic and other anxiety disorders are extremely treatable and react well to basic, short-term therapy choices.

Fortunately in recent times, an increasing number of individuals are heading to doctors and professionals about this, though some individuals are originally annoyed. When people find out they do not have a lethal condition (like a heart attack), this news might actually increase their anxiety and frustration as they begin to believe, "Well, if I am physically ALRIGHT, is anything wrong with me? I know something happened, also if I cannot quite clarify it now. What's wrong with me?"

Individuals that are undiagnosed with panic attacks or anxiety attack can discover that they jump from one medical professional to the following for months or even years without anyone being able to point to one point as well as claim, "This is the issue."

Anxiety attacks have a tendency to be on-going, ever before present feelings. Anxiety attacks are generally connected with certain fears or events. For example, if somebody is bothered about an upcoming examination, they may look at all the adverse factors in their head, over and over again, raising their anxiety and fretting about the situation. This relatively self-perpetuating condition can be classified as stress and anxiety. While it's usually not as extreme in its symptoms compared to panic disorders, it can still have a very detrimental effect on someone's life if left untended. Fortunately, awareness for these sorts of problems is growing in the clinical community, so individuals suffering are more likely than ever to be detected and effectively treated.

SYMPTOMS

The symptoms can really vary from one person to another, yet one of the most typical anxiety attack last just a few minutes, though they can last longer. Anxiety attack signs and symptoms are:

- Light-headedness and also dizziness.
- A racing and pounding heartbeat.
- Breast pains or a hefty feeling in the upper body.
- A feeling of not having the ability to capture your breath.
- Purges or chills.
- A feeling of terror.
- A feeling of blowing up.
- Feeling the anxiety of a stroke or something that will certainly cause disability.
- Fear of dying.
- Feeling anxiety about freaking out.
- Tingling in the hands, feet, legs, or arms.
- Unease noticeable by shivering or twitching muscles.
- Sweaty hands.
- Flushed face.

Common symptoms of anxiety attacks are:

- Feelings of anxiety and nervousness.
- Feeling easily inflamed.

- Feeling skeptical of your own self-esteem as well as positive self-image.
- Feeling faint or light-headed.
- Feeling disconnected from your current situation.
- An on-going feeling of despondence.
- Heavy breathing.
- Consistent crying or the feeling of requiring to cry.
- Muscle discomfort or soreness unrelated to exercise.
- Twitching, shivering, or unstable sensations in your arm or legs.
- Perspiring palms.
- Difficulty focusing or remembering points.
- A feeling of wishing to escape from your place or situation.
- A continuing focus on upsetting occasions in your very own and also other people's lives.
- Duplicating adverse conversations in your head.

There are, naturally, a variety of different problems within the brackets of panic as well as stress and anxiety. These disorders range from moderate to extreme, from sporadic to consistent. What is essential to understand is that, inevitably, they all originate from the exact same location as well as they can all be treated in a similar way.

The National Institutes of Mental Wellness (a

department of the National Institute of Health and wellness) is currently conducting a nationwide campaign to enlighten the general public as well as health care experts that panic attacks and the other anxiety conditions are some of the most effectively treated mental challenges we are facing today. A history of professional research study supplies us with a solid blueprint of cognitive, emotional, and also behavioral techniques that have actually confirmed reliability in aiding patients to conquer anxiety disorders.

As a result of the very solid, physical reactions individuals have when experiencing an anxiety attack or at the peak of a stress and anxiety assault, many individuals think there have to be a hidden condition or conditions, not connected with panic or anxiety.

The signs of an anxiety attack are very actual are because of the body's fight-or-flight response entering into overdrive. Hormones flood via the body, nerve cells fire as panic grows, and the body plans for the most awful.

This is typically along with exceptionally adverse thoughts, such as:

I assume I'm losing control.

I'm going nuts.

I have a heart attack.

I'm being smothered. I cannot breathe.

Ideas like these are frequent in the context of an anxiety attack. So don't be scared or panic, you're not alone. You're not "going crazy," as well as you are not losing control!

THE EFFECT

After experiencing an anxiety attack or a series of intense anxiety, individuals commonly discover the stress sticks around in the type of irritating concern, such as, "When will this happen to me once more? ".

Some individuals come to be so scared of having an anxiety attack (especially in public places) that they withdraw to their "secure areas." These locations have a tendency to be their residences, and they most times come to depend on that feeling of security they have in these "secure areas". Actually, many individuals rarely leave their residences whatsoever in fear of one more attack. This concern of leaving a safe place is a condition called agoraphobia. I struggled with it when anxiety, as well as panic attacks, started impacting me.

People with agoraphobia do not delight in having their life restricted; it's a disappointing and also unpleasant side effect of the condition. It's the fear of having an additional anxiety attack in public (which is an area where they do not really feel risk-free) that keeps them embedded in their home.

The results of an anxiety attack can be equally as

uncomfortable as the concern of leaving a safe place. Feelings of clinical depression and also helplessness are not uncommon. The best concern tends to be that the anxiety attack will keep coming back, making life extremely awkward.

Panic attacks are not necessarily brought on by a certain scenario. Extremely usually, the origin and also regular triggers continue to be a secret to the person suffering. Panic attacks can come "unexpectedly," yet in some cases, excessive stress or other adverse problems can likewise launch an attack.

TREATMENTS

Today, anxiety attacks, panic attack, and also agoraphobia can be dealt with not only quickly but also effectively with a series of treatments. Getting rid of panic as well as stress and anxiety does not only imply you no longer have attacks, It also suggests that you no more have the preliminary symptoms that lead you to have an anxiety attack-- the underlying cause and signs and symptoms must be gone before we claim that somebody has actually " conquered " a panic disorder.

COGNITIVE BEHAVIOR MODIFICATION

Cognitive-behavioral therapy (or CBT) is a new treatment for panic disorders and agoraphobia that has actually been shown to be really effective. Instead of utilizing traditional based treatment, experts use brand-new CBT techniques to concentrate on the current problems with panic and resolve just how to treat it.

If you experience panic as well as agoraphobia, you're not "insane," as well as you don't need to be in treatment for extended time periods. The sessions will certainly rely on the intensity of the condition as well as, of course, your determination as the client to actively join the treatment.

When a person with a panic disorder is inspired to practice and also attempt new methods, that individual is actively altering the way their mind responds. If you alter the means your mind reacts in an organized favorable means, anxiety and also panic will continue to dissipate. As time advances, the methods you make use of against it will become more powerful, and also a total absence of panic disorders can be attained.

If you insist on seeing a specialist that practices CBT, I would certainly recommend it; nonetheless, you don't require a therapist to overcome panic attacks. You can do it with breathing exercises, the right supplements, and also perseverance.

That's how I overcame my situation, and also, you can, as well.

Self-controlled breathing techniques

There are two primary means to take on panic attacks with breathing:

1. Stopping an anxiety attack when you are having one.
2. Stopping a panic attack from occurring again.

The first tactic you require to consider is how you quit an anxiety attack when you're having one. It's an effective thought. You turn off your body's fight-or-flight feedback. And also what's the most basic method to do that? I would advise making use of the 4-7-8 breath mentioned previously.

Equally, as a quick tip to save you scrolling back through the pages, here's exactly how you do it.

Sit comfortably in a straight-back position.

Expand your diaphragm as well as gradually breathe in with your nose for and count 4

Hold your breath and count 1-7

Open your mouth a little and exhale with the count of 8, getting your diaphragm.

Repeat this cycle four times.

If you follow this procedure, you should really feel that your panic attack stops, or at least decreases dramatically. If the sensations of panic persist after going through the process, just repeat for one more four rounds or up until a feeling of calmness has actually been reached. This is the method I used effectively to get my life back from an anxiety attack, and also it remains to serve to this day

To address the 2nd question of how to minimize the effect of your panic and stress and anxiety (how do you stop attacks from taking place once again), it's a daily breathing practice.

The idea behind a daily breathing practice is that your body ends up getting used to the feeling tranquil as well as relaxed. Due to this, there will certainly be less chance of your body going into fight-or-flight mode (therefore, less chance of a panic attack occurring).

It doesn't take long to discover or feel the positive impacts. It's really simple as well as there are lots of choices. My two favorites are both yoga and breathing exercises that will be explained below. (Do not worry, you don't need to understand how to bend your legs behind your back to do them!) They're basic and also reliable tools to utilize to ease the anxiety of having a panic attack ever before again.

ALTERNATE NOSTRIL BREATHING

This yoga breathing strategy creates deep relaxation with the equilibrium of the right and also left sides of the mind as the nerves are soothed.

- Sit down with both of your legs crossed or propped up on a pillow. You can likewise kneel down alongside the bed. Do not hesitate to utilize blankets or anything that can support you in order to achieve comfortability.
- Rest your left hand over your left thigh. The

fingers on your right hand should be extended as if you are attempting to swing at a person. Bend your middle and also index fingers to ensure that they crinkle inside your palm.

- Put your thumb on the side of your nose as well as a little touch your nostrils. When you touch your nostrils, be careful not to be restricting. The concept is to limit airflow momentarily to one nostril.

- Inhale deeply and after that breathe out. Close off your right nostril utilizing your thumb. Take in through your left nostril for four seconds. When you reach the peak of that breath, you ought to block your left nostril using your third finger.

- Go on the count of 4 while you hold this position to retain the breath. Release your right nostril and breathe out for 4 seconds.

- Then, take a deep breath for four seconds through your right nostril. Similar to what you did previously, shut it off, hold the placement, and maintain your breath for 4 seconds. Release your left nostril as you breathe out totally for 4 seconds. Take a deep breath with your left nostril and repeat the whole cycle.

If you can do this breathing technique as typically

as you desire, you will have a more relaxed day without having fears for panic and anxiety.

TAKE A DEEP BREATH

This breathing technique also comes from yoga. It calms the body and calms the mind. You might want to lie on a bed or on a comfortable floor for this. I suggest trying just before going to bed to help on a good night.

- Lie on your back with your legs positioned as wide as your hips. Lower your arms to the side and close your eyes.
- Breathe deeply through the nose and out through the mouth. With each breath, you must fill your lungs completely. Exhale completely with each exhalation.
- Inhale through your nose four times after three deep breaths until you narrow your throat slightly. This makes you feel like breathing through a straw in the throat and filling the lungs with air.
- You should pay attention to the sound of your breathing, mimicking the sound of incoming and outgoing waves. This sound is actually very useful for you to fall asleep. You can compare it with a quiet baby's snoring.
- Hold your breath for four seconds while watching your emotions silently. You need to try to feel calm and complete. Exhale

through your nose for four seconds when your throat is slightly narrowed.

- After your lungs have cleaned all the air, you have to start refilling.
- Take a deep breath for six seconds and hold for another six seconds.
- Finally, exhale for six seconds.
- Repeat this breathing process by adding two more seconds for each cycle.

After you reach your maximum breathing and holding capacity, you can take two seconds off for the next round. So, if you have a maximum of twelve seconds, the next round must take up to ten seconds. Reduce two seconds each time so that the next round lasts eight seconds and so on.

When you have reached four seconds, you can let go of everything and return to normal breathing. After relaxing your mind and body, you can sleep well and wake up refreshed and revitalized.

You can do this exercise in the morning, at night before going to sleep or somewhere in between. The key point is that you have to do it every day. You should pay attention to your tendency to experience anxiety and panic attacks, which decrease with time when you use it.

5

PHOBIAS

*W*hat is a phobia?

Phobias affect almost everyone. They can influence people to some extent, like the classic "public phobia" that most people don't have to face every day. Unfortunately, phobias can also affect many people, such as agoraphobia, where people find it difficult to leave home. Phobias like this can be stressful, but very treatable. And if you have a phobia, don't think that you're weird or different. There are phobias for almost everything. If you can imagine, someone has a phobia. Like aurophobia - fear of gold. tetraphobia - fear number four and its cousin Quintaphobia - fear number five.

Personally, I struggled with agoraphobia shortly after I got a panic attack. I was horrified at the thought of leaving my home in case I have another attack. So I stayed in - about three months. I lost my job because I couldn't go to work. I alienated my friends because I did not want to visit anyone. I was unhappy and bored because I felt trapped without doing anything. When I came out, I had an incredible feeling that I would fall into the sky like I was in an open space.

So far in my life, it has been as exciting as it sounds, and one day, I will have enough! I began to research everything about phobias and how to improve them. I am functioning again in a few weeks. I can leave the house. I can play soccer on a large field in the open without fear of falling to the sky. I can go out with friends without worrying about not being home.

It was incredible. It didn't take long, especially after I found out what I have to do is not as difficult as I had imagined—other things you can do in later chapters.

THE SYMPTOMS

The main difference that I want to make here is that phobias and "fears" are not necessarily the same. You can be afraid of tigers. For example, you don't want to be a steamy lunch to a hungry tiger, but you don't necessarily need to have a phobia about it. Thoughts of being eaten by tigers may not be thoughts that bother you every day.

Phobias are described as "extraordinary fears and weakening of an object, place, situation, feeling or animal." Phobias are much clearer than fear. It happens when someone has excessive or unrealistic feelings of danger from a situation or object.

When a phobia becomes very severe, you can

arrange your life around it and avoid something that scares you, like my experience.

The typical symptoms for someone with a phobia or when thinking about phobia "objects" are:

- Instability, dizziness.
- Feeling sick.
- Sweating.
- A feeling of nausea.
- Stomach upset.
- Increased heart rate and palpitations.
- Shortness of breath.

Everything is uncomfortable, but everything is very similar to the other answers we discussed. This is because these symptoms are caused by the same fight-flight response as panic attacks and other anxiety disorders.

The good news is that phobias can be treated in the same way with similar tools and techniques.

CARE

There are several ways to overcome phobias. Most of them are very uncomfortable but effective. If a phobia is something that has a negative impact on your life, working on it can be challenging, but it's worth it. This is a short chapter about some of the options available if you don't know where to start.

EXPOSURE THERAPY

The traditional method for treating phobias is exposure therapy. That's the way it sounds. Show yourself gradually to what you fear in a safe and controlled manner. During this process, the idea is that you learn to overcome fear and fear over time.

The general wisdom is that through various experiences of fear, you (and your body) will realize that the worst will not happen. With each exposure, you feel safer and more controlled. Phobias diminish and lose strength.

Successfully overcoming fear in this way requires preparation, repetition, and patience. This isn't an overnight thing, but it can be something to think about.

VISUALIZATION AND RELAXATION

This is similar to exposure therapy, but has one major advantage: You can do this comfortably from your chair!

1. Imagine what scares you. Visualize as clearly as possible.
2. Feel how your fears and emotions accumulate (the uncomfortable, but important part).
3. When you imagine how you experience

phobias and feel emotions, do calm breathing exercises, for example. B. 4-7-8 breaths.

4. Repeat 3-4 times and see if your fear decreases finally.

This technique offers all the advantages of conventional exposure therapy, but the results must be achieved faster. Its effectiveness is highly predicted for situations that can be visualized and in which the creepy emotions associated with such events can be felt as be much as possible. This is not always the easiest thing, but it is really feasible to get rid of your phobias.

6

NATURAL MEDICINE

*R*ESPONSIBILITIES. What is discussed in the following pages mainly focuses on natural supplements and over-the-counter supplements. It is always recommended that you talk with your doctor before trying one of them.

Are there any natural anxiety healing methods that can help?

Anti-anxiety supplements are becoming increasingly popular as an alternative to anxiety medications and maybe more direct than therapy or other long-term treatments. The problem with this "solution" is there are thousands. Almost every large naturopathic company has developed its own products or mixtures for the fear market. There are several problems with this "solution."

First, research shows that most natural cures for anxiety are ineffective. Another problem is when there are so many products on the market that it is very difficult to know which supplements might work and which might not.

One thing to keep in mind is that natural supplements can be a good choice for those who want to consider other treatments. But you have to admit that it's still only a temporary treatment. If you use everything else in this book, you can learn how to cope better with anxiety and take steps to cure it forever. But in the meantime, supplements can be a good thing to make you feel at home again!

Also, note that there are not as many differences between drugs and natural supplements as you might think at first. The stronger the supplement, the more likely it is to have side effects or risks (which apply to everything that changes your body chemistry). As mentioned earlier, not every fear is treated the same way. For example, panic attacks may require various types of GAD treatments. So, what works for one person may not work for you - it's important to be smart about your choices while you are reading this book!

There are one million and one things you can take, and more than one million people will tell you that their products are the best and most effective. I will tell you what works for me and what works in clinical settings.

THE BIG TWO

Two drugs that I really want to talk about are Rhodiola Rosea & L-Theanine. There are a number of studies on each of them that explain their effectiveness, as well as lots of anecdotal evidence, and after everything, I have tried - they seem to be the most effective.

RHODIOLA ROSE

Rhodiola Rosea is an herb that can be very effective in treating anxiety. Used more often as an antidepressant; however, many antidepressants are also recommended for people with anxiety, because they both work on the same neurotransmitter and signaling pathways.

This herb grows in cold regions and can have many other names, including Arctic roots, golden roots, rose roots, Aaron staff, and royal crowns. They all refer to the same small plants with yellow-flowering stems.

Rhodiola Rose is found in Russia, Scandinavia, and China. They are traditionally harvested to cope with the stresses of living in a very cold and high climate. The main effects are especially the reduction in fatigue, increased sexual potential, and enhances happiness.

In recent years, research supporting its use as an antidepressant has prompted the United States Food and Drug Administration (USFDA) to withdraw some products containing Rhodiola Rosea. There are concerns about some people who claim that the potential of this herb is to treat migraines, flu, colds, bacterial infections, and even cancer, even though this claim has been proven to be false or unsupported. Although not completely understood, Rhodiola Rosea is believed to have a combination of stimulation and relaxation properties in a ratio that makes it effective for people with depression and anxiety.

Some of the known effects of Rhodiola Rosea are:

- Decreased activity in the sympathetic nervous system. Remember that the sympathetic nervous system (SNS) takes action when a fight or flight response is triggered by the amygdala. This leads to symptoms of increased heart rate, breathing, and stress in your adrenal glands. Increased activity is responsible for all physical symptoms of anxiety, such as Rapid heartbeat, tremors, shortness of breath, dizziness, and nausea.
- Increased activity in the activity of the parasympathetic nervous system. The parasympathetic nervous system (PNS) is the opposite of SNS because it is related to slowing down the processes in the body instead of speeding them up. Increased civil servant activity will have a calming and focused effect.
- Increase in serotonin. The hormone serotonin is a neurotransmitter that is associated with happiness and relaxation.

Serotonin deficiency generally occurs in people with depression and anxiety.

- Increase memory and focus. Feeling out of focus and dazed because fear can make the fear worse, especially if you feel anxious in the midst of something as important as a meeting or exam. Various studies show that Rhodiola Rosea improves memory and focus. In a recent study using it as an aid, subjects had to do a correction test and measure their memory and focus. The results showed that patients taking Rhodiola Rosea made 88% fewer errors compared to the control group.

- Reducing recovery time after training. A common symptom of anxiety is that your heart rate tends to increase, and your breathing becomes more difficult, similar to when you exercise for a long time. Rhodiola Rosea can reduce the time needed for heart rate and breathing to return to normal. In another recent study with people who used Rhodiola Rosea before running 12 miles, the participants were tested regularly. Those who did not use Rhodiola Rosea showed an increase in impulses that were 129% higher than resting heartbeats, while the impulses from those who used Rhodiola Rosea were only 105% higher than the resting frequency.

There are fantastic reasons to try Rhodiola Rosea,

and the effects can be huge. Surely I have seen a big difference in my own life after using it. I continued to use it and admit that I helped control my anxiety and panic attacks. There are good side effects that make you feel happier and more motivated in life. Overall, this is a thumbs up for me

Should You Use Rhodiola Rosea?

After all, it's cheap, safe, and effective for hundreds of years. I would definitely suggest taking something and trying it. If that doesn't work for you, that's fine. There are hundreds of other things to try, but it can be the most effective supplement you will ever take to fight anxiety.

THEANINE

Theanine is a common compound found mainly in green or black tea. This is a supplement that is widely used and can be an effective tool for relieving anxiety. Theanine improves the function of your body naturally and effectively.

I initially discovered it when experiments with green tea caused extraction. Interestingly, black tea can sometimes contain as much green tea, because both green and black tea come from the same plant, Camellia sinensis. The only difference is that black tea is heat-treated and sometimes fermented before drying.

It also seems to stimulate brain dopamine, one of the neurotransmitters "feeling good." This can be the main reason why most people report being fully focus and strong mental concentration after the use of Theanine.

Is Theanine Effective in Overcoming Anxiety?

There is some research on this, and although there are no definite clinical studies, many (including me) have seen that it really helps reduce their anxiety. This can also have a profound effect on improving sleep quality.

There are a number of interesting studies showing that Theanine can increase alpha wave activity in the brain, where alpha waves are an indicator of brain resting at rest. Most of these studies have not been done with people suffering from anxiety. However, usually, people who tend to worry naturally have fewer alpha waves and more beta wave activity (which is usually related to alertness and attention).

Other studies have shown that Theanine has helped reduce stress responses in people exposed to stressful conditions under experimental conditions. These studies have not been conducted on anxiety patients, but stress reduction or improvement in stress management is likely to help combat and manage anxiety for someone who does it.

Can I drink tea?

Since I am, you will not be surprised to hear that drinking a glass of tea is my top choice for all types of treatments. Although drinking Theanine tea certainly gives a little push, the amount is unfortunately not standard and can vary greatly. Expected doses can range from 5 mg per cup of tea (hot or frozen, irrelevant) to 46 mg per cup of high-quality gourmet tea.

So, even though it's not perfect, you can drink a glass of tea to get your Theanine. As mentioned earlier, black tea also contains Theanine, but the main difference is nothing irrespective of whether the tea is green or black. Tea leaves are very young at harvest time. Theanine is found in the highest concentration in shoots and young leaves of tea plants.

Because of the additional costs of harvesting these teas, they are more expensive. Tea like Matcha, Sencha, and Gyokuro can be many times more expensive than an ordinary cup of tea. Oolong and Darjeeling teas are other types of gourmet teas that tend to have high theanine concentrations because they are obtained from young tea plants.

This still leaves the question of how much you should take Theanine every day.

How much should be taken?

Theanine has been shown to have therapeutic benefits at doses between 50 and 200 mg. With this amount, you need to drink five to ten cups of normal tea to get the same dose of Theanine when taking a small capsule. This is not a problem for me because I would consider at least five glasses a day, but I don't think this is normal for anyone outside the UK.

Useful additions here. Theanine small package can be purchased for around $ 10 and lasts for several months. Most doses are usually standardized up to 100 mg per capsule, so you can use the daily "test" procedure to determine exactly how much Theanine is right for you.

Start with 100 mg and see how you are doing. If you like how you feel, maybe try a little more. If not, give a small dose. Doses up to 250 mg per day is considered safe, according to the FDA, and higher doses are not needed for anyone I know who has used them.

Theanine has a relatively short half-life (which means that your body metabolizes for about 2.5-4.5 hours), but in my experience, the morning dose is sufficient for the whole day.

There are many types! Who buys?

Theanine is an amino acid, even though it is not part of the protein. Like all amino acids, Theanine is available in two mirror forms: "L" and "D." You might see that it is sold as L-theanine versus D-theanine. The first is the active version, and D-theanine has no effect on your brain. (So L-Theanine is what you want!)

However, you can see some products that are only called "theanine" without "L". This occurs when Theanine is synthesized in a laboratory. The result is a mixture of L-theanine (which we want) and D-theanine (which we don't care about). Separation of L-theanine itself increases efforts. Many manufacturers can cut corners and only use mixtures as they are.

The company uses a patented fermentation process that mimics the natural production of theanine in tea leaves. Because of this special process, it approaches "naturally produced theanine," as you might find.

Despite all this extraordinary, extracting pure L-theanine from tea leaves is actually very expensive. As a result, most commercially available L-theanine is not extracted in the same way. If you really don't mind spending more money to ensure the purity and quality of L-theanine, just look for Suntheanine supplements.

However, L-Theanine can be clean and high quality from other leading companies. The only thing to remember is that cheaper brands tend not to try to ensure the purity and ratio of L-theanine and D-theanine because they are much cheaper to produce. So you can't be sure how much you get.

Do I have to try Theanine?

Theanine seems to be one of the more useful supplements that you can use to deal with anxiety. The worst risk is that it might not help you much or not at all. It does not have the same powerful effects as some drugs, but it is not risky.

In my opinion, if you try Theanine, you can function properly without feeling calm. You will not risk retreating or restoring fear if you no longer accept it. Theanine can be a fantastic addition to relieve some anxiety symptoms and can be an integral part of your self-care.

Is there anyone who shouldn't use Theanine?

Theanine has been widely studied in toxicology and clinical studies in a laboratory environment. Side effects appear to have never been reported in the general population or in laboratory studies for nearly 50 years. The only side effect that might occur for years is a headache, but it has been reported to occur only at very high doses.

L-theanine is approved by the FDA in the United States as a supplement in doses of up to 250 mg. It is also known as GRAS (commonly known as safe). However, there are several things to consider.

If you are pregnant or breastfeeding, consult your doctor first. This should be done without saying, but I will say it: if you take the prescribed medication, the time not to worry, then first discuss the supplement you are considering using with your doctor. ,

My main warning when I say that anyone can try it comes with diagnosed depression or when you are prone to episodes of depression. You must be very careful if you take something that increases the level of GABA in your brain.

GABA

If you have anxiety, an increase in GABA levels in your brain has a dramatic effect. GABA is a neurotransmitter that occurs naturally in your brain, and low levels appear to be very closely related to several types of anxiety. In this case, it makes sense that you want to increase your GABA levels if you want to reduce your anxiety.

Theanine intake can be an inexpensive and effective way to increase GABA levels. Theanine not only increases GABA but also works synergistically by weakening a number of stimulating neurotransmitters that make you anxious. You might think: "If GABA is very good, why don't I take it?" Unfortunately, that is not always easy.

Some people get good results from taking GABA supplements. The main problem is that it does not cross the blood-brain barrier very effectively; This means that most of the GABA in supplements do not reach your goal - and we cannot measure how much GABA is absorbed. Therefore, regulating GABA levels in the brain through direct supplementation can be very difficult.

Now there are some fantastic GABA pills that use very interesting techniques to overcome them, such as companies that bind GABA molecules to liposomes (fat molecules) so they can be absorbed and absorbed more efficiently. The only problem is that the price is very high. If you have money to burn, check. If not, the answer might be Theanine.

Interestingly, Theanine crosses the blood-brain barrier quite well. It usually has the same effect as increasing GABA in your brain, so it can be a very quick and easy way to do the same thing.

SYNERGISTIC SUPPLEMENTS

Like food supplements derived from plants, tea can provide additional ingredients that we have not identified. Some of these ingredients can work with Theanine to enhance their effects.

The most important thing we know is caffeine. Tea seems to have a very positive interaction with Theanine, and you are far less likely to get caffeine than with coffee. Unfortunately, caffeine might not be too good for most people with anxiety. I certainly saw a dramatic increase in anxiety and panic attacks when I eliminated caffeine from my diet. Let's look more closely in the next chapter.

7

STAYING AWAY FROM CAFFEINE

*W*hile the last section examines which supplements work well for reducing anxiety, it's important to remember that some of the things you take can have a negative impact on your anxiety. Caffeine is really annoying for me and has proven to be a good trigger for my concerns. And I have learned that it is a very common trigger for anxiety and panic attacks.

How do I know that caffeine is exacerbating my fear?

I like coffee. I have for years. I like the smell, I like the complexity of the scent, and I like the way it wakes me up in the morning. In the past few years, my mornings always begin with a good cup of coffee, and sometimes I drink double espresso later when extra encouragement is needed.

When I started experiencing anxiety problems and panic attacks, I read everything I could and learned that there was a lot of evidence that caffeine could increase and sometimes even cause anxiety. I clearly think I was one of the lucky ones who didn't become a problem because I drank it long before this problem occurred, so that wasn't the reason. Of course, I'm fine with caffeine but after several months of constant panic attacks and fears, I decided to try to stop the caffeine for a few days to see if it made a difference.

The first day I did not have coffee to start my morning. It's a little harder to keep going, and of course, I yawned several times more than usual, but ... I didn't experience panic attacks and anxiety.

So the next day, I did the same: no coffee and no fear. On the third day, I decided to get my morning caffeine back. Very delicious. I missed it. I miss the smell. I miss the taste. What I didn't miss were the fear and panic attacks that I experienced this morning.

Now I know it can be a doll. Correlation does not have to be identical to causal relations. So I tried to extend the caffeine experiment to two full weeks. During this time, I no longer had problems with panic attacks and drastically reduced my constant fear.

At the end of two weeks, I was given a coffee gift... You must remember this experience. Fear increased, and within a few hours after drinking a good cup of coffee, I experienced a panic attack.

Since then, I have done my best to avoid high doses of caffeine, and it is definitely a good machine to reduce my anxiety. Annoyingly, everything seems to contain caffeine: headache medication, soda, even tea. However, tea does not seem to have a negative effect. I assume it's due to the reduced caffeine content compared to coffee and very calming compounds like theanine.

GIVING CAFFEINE

Now you might be thinking,

Wow, you should immediately stop caffeine!

You are more like,

There is no way to stop caffeine! This is not bad for me; I have been drinking it for years! How do I go without it in the morning? I will fall asleep on my desk!

Now look, I will not ignore it. Walking with cold turkey caffeine is associated with some of the more unpleasant experiences of my life, and I definitely want to avoid doing it again if possible. I have a headache, feel tired, unhappy... but I don't have panic attacks, so overall it is a plus.

The good news is that you can take full advantage of avoiding caffeine-free turkey without any drawbacks. All you have to do is reduce it gradually.

THE PLAN

Before discussing all these plans, try a decaffeinated day first. This is not coffee, tea, soda, energy drinks, or anything with caffeine hidden in it. If you see an improvement in your symptoms or feel a positive benefit, you owe it to yourself to try to lose caffeine, if only for a short time.

This is very easy. All you have to do is gradually reduce your caffeine intake every day for one or two weeks.

Here I will use coffee as an example because it is the most famous source of caffeine for many people.

- **Day 1**: Simply drink your normal coffee.
- **Days 2-5**: Mix your coffee with about 50% decaf. Drink this until the end of day 5.
- **Day 6**: Mix 25% of your normal coffee with 75% of coffee without caffeine in one day.
- **Day 7**: Only drink coffee without caffeine.

CONGRATULATIONS! You officially drink coffee now!

If you experience it and don't see improvement, you are one of the lucky ones who can drink caffeine without problems! Take a glass of Joe and enjoy your morning. However, if you are like most people or me, you might see a significant improvement if you don't consume caffeine. In this case, it's easier than you think to live without caffeine.

HOW TO LIVE WITHOUT CAFFEINE

There are several ways to replace caffeinated drinks so you can stick to your plan.

- Decaffeinated soft drinks - easy to read when you read the label.
- Carbonated water - this is the flavor you get, but the most amazing! They make fruit juices taste natural and other things.
- Coffee without caffeine - When you get a good brand, it tastes good! And you can enjoy it later tonight without affecting your sleep.

The only thing I haven't found is a good substitute for energy drinks. This is basically a caffeinated beverage. So stick to carbonated water if you can. Otherwise, decaffeinated soft drinks work best if you need a flavored foam drink with sweet juice or fruit.

ANOTHER BENEFIT OF ELIMINATING CAFFEINE

So you are still wondering whether to reduce caffeine or not. I understand that it's hard to think about because it's been so involved throughout our lives. If the thought of eliminating your anxiety at night is not enough for you, there are several other reasons that you should consider to eliminate caffeine.

SAVINGS

This coffee can add up to thousands of dollars a day.

- Grande Starbucks Latte: $ 3.65 per day $ 26 per week $ 1,332 a year
- 5 hours of energy: $ 3 per day $ 21 per week $ 1,095 per year
- Homemade Coffee: $ 0.71 per day $ 5 a week $ 259 a year
- Monster Energy Drink: $ 3 per day, $ 21 per week $ 1,095 per year
- K cups: $ 0.65 per day $ 4.55 per week $ 237 a year

This is some pretty serious savings. Think about what you can do with these extra bonuses a year!

LOWER YOUR BLOOD PRESSURE

Caffeine has been shown to increase your blood pressure. Cutting caffeine can lower blood pressure and maintain your heart health longer.

Better sleep

Caffeine can significantly affect the quality of your sleep. If you drink coffee or other caffeinated drinks in the afternoon, you might not be able to fall asleep because caffeine stays in your system for four to six hours.

Getting rid of caffeine at least after 12 pm is a good idea, and you should pay attention to a significant improvement in your sleep quality.

A better mood

Caffeine changes your mood. It is not uncommon for people to say that they mumble until they drink coffee in the morning and feel weak when it runs out in the afternoon.

If you stop caffeine completely, you will no longer experience these ups and downs. You can have constant energy throughout the day, without crashes and without growls.

White and healthier teeth

It is known that coffee and tea can stain your teeth. Energy and soft drinks are just as bad and can erode tooth enamel and cause damage.

Removing it will make you healthier and (some say more importantly) whiter teeth.

Significant weight los

Caffeinated drinks usually add empty calories to our food, which we don't use in any way. Many experts say that sugary drinks are an important factor in the obesity epidemic.

See what you can save by cutting this caffeinated beverage.

- If you break the habit of "one energy drink a day," you save 200 calories a day, 1400 calories a week, and 73,000 calories a year!
- If you release "one Starbucks Vanilla Latte a day," save 250 calories a day, 1750 calories a week, and 91 250 calories a year!

Are you kidding? More than 90,000 calories a year? The following is a simple marker

Row: "Cut the vanilla latte and take out the stomach".

No more flashing

One of the main side effects experienced by caffeine sufferers is nervousness or shaking hands. This can be a minor or major inconvenience. Giving up can either calm your steady hands or accelerate your progress toward a healthier self.

Reduces the risk of heart problems

Caffeine stimulates the heart muscle and makes the

heartbeat with stronger contractions. People with underlying heart disease can be at risk. Also, keep in mind that an increase in muscle pressure can be associated with an increase in pressure on the inner blood vessels and weakening of the walls of the arteries.

Reducing the risk of type 2 diabetes

Black coffee can actually reduce the risk of diabetes. Unfortunately, most people don't usually drink black coffee. According to the Harvard School of Public Health, sugar coffee, or caffeinated drinks can actually increase the risk of diabetes by up to 26%.

As you can see, reducing caffeine has a number of advantages. No need to be permanent with an Easy Cancellation Plan, it's not even difficult. Try it, you owe it to yourself!

8

USEFUL SUPPLEMENTS

*I*f you choose Rhodiola Rosea or Theanine, you will see a significant decrease in anxiety. If you are successful and want to know what is still effective, you can try some of the other options listed in this chapter.

Food supplements can be great tools for dealing with anxiety, but they may not be your only means. The key is to get your fear under control first, and then work to eliminate it forever. This is something that requires a little more work than taking some extra vitamins in the morning, but it is very achievable.

Below are the most commonly used anti-anxiety supplements, broken down into their main categories, and little information about performance.

HERBAL INTERVENTIO

Herbal supplements are the most common type available. Many believe that the right herbs can give your body the same drug effects like other drugs, but with the added benefit of fewer side effects because they are usually available without a prescription. The most popular herbal supplements are:

- **Coffee** - one of the most commonly used food supplements and scientifically researched to deal with anxiety. This is one of the few herbal supplements whose research has proven to be cheaper compared to traditional anxiety medications. It's good to consider this as a supplement, but keep in mind that coffee must interact with alcohol and other drugs. This is also related to liver damage, but it this is common, especially, in people who drink alcohol regularly.
- **Passionflower** - sometimes referred to as a soaked version of coffee, but has the advantage of not having the same alcohol interaction problem. Passionflower is not generally considered strong enough for some of the more serious anxiety disorders but can be a useful tool for people with manageable anxiety.
- **Valerian root** - traditionally used to support sleep, its relaxing effect has a good effect on

anxiety. Valerian root is similar to passionflower because it has a noticeable effect, but it might not be strong enough if you have a panic attack. It's more useful to focus or help you fall asleep on a stressful day if you are worried about something.

There may be thousands of other herbal supplements that you can think of, but these are the only ones that I have experience with and good success rate. Herbal teas such as chamomile and mint can also produce results. However, keep in mind that the results can mostly be in the form of a placebo.

VITAMINS AND OTHER SUPPLEMENTS

Vitamins and alternative nutritional supplements are becoming increasingly popular as a potential treatment for anxiety. Unfortunately, there is inadequate research on the benefits of additives and their effects on anxiety levels.

Nevertheless, it is very well documented that the lack of certain vitamins can cause fear. It has not been clinically proven that supplements can have significant anti-anxiety effects.

However, supplements with vitamins can be beneficial regardless of your health. So try one or more of them. The most common are:

- **Magnesium** - Recent studies have shown

that millions of people are becoming increasingly popular as a result of treatment for deficiency due to changes in their mineral content in terms of food and eating habits. Because magnesium affects the health of nerves, blood cells, and so on, there is good reason to believe that low magnesium levels can be an important factor in some troublesome symptoms. It's also good enough for your health, so try it.

- **GABA** - **GABA** is a major neurotransmitter inhibitor that slows your effects and calms you down. It can be bought as an additive. Unfortunately, as I mentioned before, standard type cans. GABA supplements are not believed to cross the blood-brain barrier, so it is unlikely to have a strong effect. You can use a GABA derivative called Phenibut, but this preparation can have side effects. So I really wouldn't recommend doing it without your own extensive research.

- **5-HTP** - has been popular with people who have tried to cure their anxiety and depression for some time. It helps the body synthesize serotonin and melatonin (both are calming and good for the brain). There are a number of studies that show the benefits of 5-HTP, but most have not been done well. The results must be taken with a pinch of salt. Even so, many people swear that it can also work for you.

- **Melatonin** - one of the main hormones that cause sleep. This is pumped to the brain before going to sleep and helps you relax. Fortunately, this is available as a food supplement. Because of its effectiveness and possible inhibition of natural melatonin production, some countries require a prescription for melatonin. There hasn't been much research specifically focusing on the effects of melatonin on anxiety, but many people repeat it as one of their favorite supplements.

- **Vitamin B** - the most common vitamin on the market. All vitamins can reduce anxiety. Vitamin B is an important element in the nervous system; therefore research shows that vitamin B supplements can also improve anxiety symptoms.

Different vitamins are more effective for different people. It depends on your diet, environment, and genetics. However, most vitamins are unlikely to have side effects if consumed in the amount recommended by health institutions such as the FDA. Although you still need to discuss this with your doctor before taking vitamin supplements, you might consider trying a few of them and see what benefits you get from them.

HOMEOPATHIC ALTERNATIVES

Call me skeptical, but I haven't seen many results that shows that homeopathy works ... as is. I have not talked to anyone who succeeded with him.

In fact, there is little evidence that homeopathic medicine has an effect, and most beliefs about homeopathy differ directly from modern science. Not that this is a bad thing (because the original scientific era was that the earth was flat), so I'm glad I was wrong if it worked.

However, homeopathic medicines don't seem to have a risk, so you can check various methods to determine whether they meet your needs.

9

UNUSUAL SOLUTIONS

*B*reathing exercises and natural supplements alone can solve the problem of anxiety for most people. They are very powerful, so I want to write a book to help as many people as possible and share my experiences with what helps me. But what other options do you have?

If you don't want to do breathing exercises or take supplements, what other options are available to treat your anxiety?

DRUG

In the western world, drugs seem to be the most popular choice. I strongly disagree with the spread of panic drugs, anxiety, and related disorders, but it seems that it is the solution for many people.

I have mentioned several times in this book that you should visit your doctor if you are considering taking supplements, changing your diet, etc. I think it is important that you contact a doctor hope that when you are considering the use of medications for your anxiety.

If you want to find a doctor who is open to other treatments, there are several lists made by people to help everyone choose the right doctor for them.

I am here to tell you that you can make big changes to your own heart without the need for a doctor.

Yes, if you are sick, call your doctor. Yes, if you cannot resolve your anxiety using the steps in this book, go to your doctor, but please don't continue to take medication alone because this is an easy way out. No, I promise you.

DIET

"You are what you eat." We've all heard of it. Usually, this is a well-meaning comment from someone trying to distract you from French fries and burgers for something greener and healthier.

I refused to do it, especially when I was young. I think I can eat whatever I want (usually a big bowl of pasta) and I can be fine. And it was like that for a while.

Many things have changed since then, and I am not the same person as me. I get better every day and work for big goals, but at that moment, this lazy mindset makes sense to me.

The point is, when I was young and lost my job, I went to the routine of sleeping a lot, waking up, eating a big bowl of pasta, and then feeling tired, categorized, and not inspired for the rest of the day.

I sleep 12-13 hours a day and am still tired all the time. What is this about? Not surprisingly, this "wasted life" happened when anxiety and depression came to visit me. Accidental? I think not.

I found a sudden change in energy, and my fear disappeared when I found work and started to eat better at work. My depression is gone. I am happier because I am healthier. As you can see from the section headings, my opinion on this topic is very important: **You are what you eat**.

TAKE YOU, GO!

There is a lot of research on how bacteria in the intestines affect your mood, and there is a lot of research on how different foods affect your feelings.

As a simple example, what happens when you have a big lunch? I'm talking a few sandwiches or maybe pasta, carbonated drinks, and a chocolate chip or two in the end. Now tell me how you feel about an hour after that?

Do you feel like sleeping and can't think clearly? Do you feel a little slow for the rest of the day? Most likely. (If not, you are a kind of medical anomaly and can make good sales of your body in science.)

This is just a very simple example of how food can directly affect your mind and physiology. So it's not too stressful if this additional dose of sugar at lunch can dramatically affect you so that the suboptimal diet can contribute to other things in the long run, namely anxiety and panic attacks.

We already know that excess carbohydrates cause obesity (don't worry, this won't be a diet book). With the growth of obesity throughout the world, we have seen a strong association with an increase in neurodegenerative diseases such as Alzheimer's, which many scientists have classified as type 3 diabetes because they are the result of insulin resistance in the brain.

However, science then says that excess carbohydrates in large quantities can seriously damage your mind and body for years. BUT ... the good news is you can always do something. The answer seems to be to eat fewer carbohydrates and a higher, healthy fat diet.

Why is that important, you ask? We gradually see strong evidence of healthy fats that improve cognitive function in Alzheimer's patients.

If you are not enthusiastic about this statement, the same concept applies to other fields of medicine. There are a number of scientists who are truly enthusiastic about the fact that a diet low in carbohydrates and high in fat (known as the "ketogenic" diet) seems to have a profound effect on inflammation in the body, as well as a number of other beneficial ones. Things.

I tried a ketogenic diet for a month. And I don't have panic attacks. Then I started eating carbohydrates again, and they came back.

As I mentioned before, I also experimented with caffeine elimination. (By the way, coffees, I will definitely not stop drinking tea.) I have made some very profound results with my changes. No more caffeine = no more fear.

Now I don't want this chapter to be a useful low-carb lifestyle because you will find lots of books and blogs that claim to be the best since sliced bread (pun intended). What I want to show you is that what you eat can really affect your feelings. So if I say try to get rid of caffeine for 30 days and see your anxiety subside, I know it will work.

This whole chapter is about showing you this. What you put in your body also has a strong impact on your fears and panic reactions.

So eat better and feel better!

PRACTICE

If there is one thing that is agreed to by the medical community, it is good practice. You can also agree that a lack of exercise is bad. Many studies show a very strong relationship between lack of physical activity and the possibility of developing anxiety disorders. Although not everyone can agree on the right reasons, there are several reasons agreed upon:

- **Increased stress hormones.** When you are stressed, your body releases the main stress hormone, cortisol. Many studies have shown that exercise helps to control cortisol levels and bring about balance in the brain's neurotransmitter levels. This is a link to what we discussed earlier in this book. Anxiety is an external symptom of fighting or running. When your body experiences it, it expects you to fight or escape from something. If you don't do anything, your body doesn't know what to do with itself, thereby increasing production to make you act.

- **Unused energy.** You are forced to move, and if your body does not move, it can create tension. You might notice this in animals. Dogs are very sensitive, and you will find that if they don't walk around every day, they can become anxious and strong. The concept is really the same. This is because they do not use up their energy, and then there is physical tension first and then mental tension.

- **Balance of the immune system.** Exercise is also a key factor in maintaining a regular immune system and maintaining a healthy hormonal balance in the brain and body. Some research shows that the absence of action can prevent this balance.

Apart from these highlights, secondary factors can occur. Inactive people tend to spend less time enjoying the experience, and positive experiences can help reduce anxiety. People who don't work to improve their health can develop negative health problems that can also cause anxiety.

Regardless of the mechanism, it's not good for you not to exercise.

Obviously, a lack of exercise is not the only reason for everyone to worry. Some people may be genetically predisposed to experience anxiety. Other people have traumatic experiences that have developed their anxiety symptoms. Regardless of whether not actively causing your fear or not, there are many studies that say exercise can be one of the best ways to overcome it.

So, what is in me?

If you have not thought of it, let me try to sell you the benefits. Exercise itself can be an effective treatment to reduce or even eliminate your anxiety suddenly. Every physical activity will help eliminate anxiety, and the more exercise you do, the more likely you will see results.

I know that the thought of regular exercise is disappointing for many people. It's uncomfortable to think about something you might have tried and failed before. But now you have more reasons to do it. You run not only along this road to get fit for the beach, but also to overcome your fears! That's a pretty good motivator, right?

Exercise is a very effective way to manage your anxiety every day. Movement can be a medicine for many people. For others, practice will be part of a broader strategy for dealing with anxiety. At least it will be very helpful, and therefore you will be healthier.

Overcoming your fear is about using tools and techniques to improve your quality of life. Movement is undoubtedly one of the most powerful tools for this purpose. Some of the benefits that you should expect from regular exercise are:

- Generally healthy. There's a reason why you're happier when you're fine, right? Right.
- Being less active doesn't make sense, right? If you exercise regularly, all the negative consequences of being inactive including anxiety are no longer a problem. Even if inactivity is not the original cause of your anxiety, it can make the problem worse. Regular exercise has a drastic effect on problems that occur during inactivity.
- More neurotransmitters "get well soon." One of the main reasons why exercise acts as an effective solution to reduce anxiety is that exercise releases natural chemicals in your body and brain that have effects similar to some artificial anxiety medications. You will find exercises that release endorphins in your brain that act as natural painkillers for your body. Endorphins are usually released to prevent movements causing pain, but they also play a major role in regulating mood (getting better) and calming the mind. Really

all we want from treatment, but without side effects!

- Cortisol reduction. Anyone who is afraid tends to have excess cortisol in his body. This is because of the pressure caused by fear on them. Exercise has the amazing effect of lowering cortisol and eliminating so many symptoms that can cause further anxiety, such as problems with concentration and fatigue.

Sleep better. If you have practiced hard, you know that sleeping that night will be much easier. Your body is tired and needs time to rest and recover. Because falling asleep can fight many anxiety states, exercise can be a good natural way to encourage sleep faster and improve sleep quality. Improving sleep quality has a big impact on everyone who is afraid because your body has time to really rest and relax.

And a few more.

- Less stress, stress, and mental fatigue.
- Increased energy naturally.
- Feeling of success.
- Focus on life and motivation.
- Not angry or faint.
- Healthy appetite.
- Better social life.
- Having fun!

There are a million other reasons why exercise decreases your anxiety. Exercise increases self-confidence. It's healthy for your bod, and good physical health is very important for maintaining a healthy mind. It helps every aspect of your body work more effectively and improves balance in your body.

So, what should I do?

When most people hear,

Hey, you have to start exercising and feel great

they usually think,

Yes, yes, I've heard of it before, but I've never been able to follow a routine. It's long. Exercise isn't for me.

If you haven't practiced for some time, it might be difficult to get used to... but it's not as difficult as living with fear for the rest of your life!

When you start for the first time, it gets harder before it gets easier. Your body must be familiar with the effort. What you will find in one or two weeks is that you can train harder longer, with less stress on your breathing and more endorphins that taste good! The good news is that you don't need to exercise hard. You just need to move more.

I definitely think that you should focus on more intensive practice. Some of the main benefits of exercise require that you make your body adapt and change, but any sport is better than not exercising.

Even if it only runs 20 minutes or you play basketball once a day, you will clearly see the difference in your fears.

How do I get started?

Sports should not be too complex. In fact, you don't need to feel like moving at all. You can start by just taking a walk. The most important thing is you just move. Find something to follow, and then make sure you do it every day.

If walking isn't your thing, there are almost unlimited choices.

- Take a bicycle and go anywhere - I use my bicycle to go home and work. Save me a lot of gas!
- Sports - soccer or basketball. Whatever your favorite sport, go and play! Have fun, and start.
- Exercising at home - There are probably hundreds of fitness channels on YouTube with exercise programs that you can do at home, usually without additional equipment. They can be very effective and best of all; they are free!
- Running - You don't have to try running a marathon directly from the gate. Start by running short on the road and come back and build your stamina.

- Weightlifting - visiting a fitness center can be a scary thing, but you don't have to go right in. You can work until you become healthier!
- Fitness classes - If you exercise weight lifting, it is better to take classes offered in most gyms. Starting from circuit training to spinning, dancing, and others. Find what sounds like fun, and keep going!
- Swimming - You don't need to want to be Michael Phelps to swim. This is a good and fun exercise. As an added bonus, exposure to cold water can help you burn fat!
- Yoga - If you don't like to move, but still want to increase your heart rate, yoga and stretching can be a great way to do this.

After all, it's all about movement. If you use your muscles and your heart beats a little faster (even if it is a low-intensity exercise), you will have a big impact on reducing your anxiety symptoms.

How Much Should I Exercise?

A general guideline for adults is to aim for about 150 minutes of moderate activity each week. This requires an average of 30 minutes, five times a week. This might sound like a lot at first, but even a 15-minute walk can help clear your mind and relax.

In the end, all your training leads to more intensive training because the higher the intensity of the exercise, the more benefits you will get from it, and the more positive your fear will be. As always, I would recommend talking to your doctor before starting an exercise program - especially if you plan to do this intensively.

The main distance from all this is; Every exercise is better than nothing.

AFFIRMATION

That might sound a bit out but just follow along now. So much depression and anxiety revolve around negative thought patterns. Among other things, we discuss positive affirmations to combat this.

Using affirmations might sound a little "new" or pointless, but I'm willing to bet that every successful person you've ever heard of uses it to be successful. And hey, if it's good enough for Dale Carnegie, that's good enough for us, right?

The funny thing is, you already used confirmation. Everyone does it; they don't always realize it. All this silence you do, the things you say to yourself, are your own inner affirmation. Every time you say things like:

- *What if something happens to me?*
- *I'll be embarrassed in public.*
- *My heart is racing; I'm going to die.*
- *There is something wrong.*
- *I'm not a happy person.*

This is an example of an affirmation, not a good one! But don't worry; that is not your fault. Even people who are not afraid often have very negative self-talk. Most people are not aware of their own conversations, but it has an impact on their lives.

In fact, the results we get are based on what we think. You get more from things that capture your focus. If you focus on bad things, you will find more bad things. But if you focus on the good things, you will see more than that!

HOW TO USE AFFIRMATIONS TO OVERCOME FEAR

So we found that you already have the confirmation that you are using. You might just use it unconsciously. We will replace this negative statement with a positive one.

The whole idea of affirmation is that they must repeat themselves consistently, as you have done unconsciously. Now you want to repeat positive affirmations instead.

Your affirmations must be positive and reflective and usually describe your feelings. As an example:

- *My fear doesn't control me.*
- *I'm safe and secure.*
- *I feel peaceful and at peace.*
- *I have a great life, and I will continue to live a great life.*

- *I know I can stop my panic attacks.*

You can use it if you are worried, but repeating it every day is the most effective way to use it. Find what you like online, from friends, or write your own. Read it every morning. You can have as much or as much as you want, whatever works for you.

Overcome the attitude "I do not believe in this nonsense."

If you don't have experience using confirmation, it seems silly at first. It's hard to say things that are not true, that you are not sure whether you believe in the hope that will help you overcome fear. The purpose of affirmations is not to trust them miraculously or to immediately cure your stress and anxiety. The real purpose of affirmations is to take the power of negative voices in your head. All the time you spend repeating your positive affirmations is a time when negative thoughts cannot bother you.

Affirmations can have a profound effect while taking a little time. You have several other advantages:

- Produces positive interference. Fear is something that can stop and worsen when your mind is pounding. So your coping tools must be positive and uplifting. If you use affirmations, you have the option to repeat this type of value for yourself. This will temporarily divert your fear and help you focus on great ideas.

- Repetition leads to faith. Your brain continues to adapt to new stimuli. If he doesn't understand something, he changes it to fit it. Repeating positive phrases that conflict with negative thoughts that you normally think will cause your brain to adapt to new beliefs that you repeat. This practice is based on the theory of cognitive dissonance, a very common phenomenon that is often described with things like important actors. Actors sometimes feel like their characters. Fortunately, you can take advantage of this by getting the same benefits through confirmation.

- Strengthen positivity. It is a big advantage of affirmations to function as a reminder to be positive and to feel positive. They can be a good reminder of how you want to feel and what you work for.

The claim is rooted in the idea of neurolinguistic programming or NLP. In this context, it is believed that positive confirmation, which is repeated sequentially, can change a person's brain chemistry in ways that promote healing and positivity. NLP has doubts in the scientific community but has a steady following all over the world. I personally have a very positive experience with it, and if not, at least there are no side effects!

HOW TO MAXIMIZE THE VALUE OF ANNOTATIONS

Your statement itself must be an expression that is important to you. If you search online, you can find hundreds of examples, and this can be a good place to start. Ideally, confirmation should be something written in your own words that is personal to you. That way, it means more to you when you read it and has more effects.

For a certificate to be valid, you must also read it continuously. Given how it works, you won't see the great benefit of validating the right way. You might feel a little silly and uncomfortable reading these things for the first time, but keep using them!

Affirmations become more effective, the longer you use them. Your discomfort will decrease as you read it, making it feel more natural and more effective. Once again, remember that affirmation is not an independent treatment for anxiety but can be an integral part of self-medication.

So what can I say?

Now that you understand the benefits of affirmations, it is time to give you several examples to help you get started!

You can use the list below or search the Internet for examples that you think are suitable for getting started. You don't have to use it. You just have to choose which one suits you. There is no minimum amount of confirmation required. Just go with what you want.

Example confirmation:

- I'm cool and calm.
- Every breath I breathe in soothes me, and every breath I breathe out sends away tension.
- Every cell in my body is calm and relaxed.
- I am very loving and unconditional.
- I am confident that I will succeed in solving life's problems.
- I live in peace. I can handle all types of stress.
- I am social and like to meet people.
- Everything is good in my world, and I'm safe.
- With each breath, I am calmer.
- With each breath, I release fear in myself.
- The future is positive. I am happy with hope and happiness in my heart.
- I constantly overcome my fears and live my life bravely.
- I understand that the only constant in life changes, and I am always ready for it.
- I am free from fear and live my life to the fullest.

WHEN TO USE AFFIRMATIONS

As mentioned before, confirmation must be repeated every day to be effective. Morning is usually the easiest.

It's easiest to read before or after brushing your teeth. That way, you will be reminded to do it every morning, and soon they will become part of your morning routine so you will not forget to do it.

The only important thing is the confirmation must be readout. With that in mind, most people want to do it when they are alone, so they don't feel like talking crazy! Another reason to do it together with brushing your teeth is a good thing because you are alone in a separate room, so you can feel safer when reading.

Ugh! That's a lot of information. I hope you have found the best chapters and tools for you, and that have added value to this book.

Don't worry if you still feel a little overwhelmed with all this information! This is very easy. Just follow these steps, and you are heading for ways to overcome fear.

ACTION PLAN

1. Learn to use 4-7-8 breaths to deal with anxiety.
2. Try taking natural supplements like Rhodiola Rosea or L-Theanine.
3. Stop consuming caffeine (don't forget the Easy Caffeine Cessation Plan).
4. Follow exercises that you can do every day.
5. Write positive affirmations and read every day.

That is. Simple steps to get at least most of the way there and significantly reduce your ongoing anxiety. You might be able to stop panic attacks and feel happier in your life!

However, there is always something you can do to improve your life. In this book, you will learn how to regain control of your life. Then it's up to you what you do with your freedom!

10

GET INVOLVED IN THE REAL WORLD

*I*n the last ten years, technology has penetrated every area of our lives. You might remember a time like me when there were no smartphones or even cellphones, no laptops, no social media, or email. The advent of this technology has brought many benefits, such as rapid exchange of ideas and the ability to connect quickly and easily to people around the world.

At the same time, technology everywhere has potential weaknesses. Many research studies have begun to examine the effects of various technologies on our well-being. Your results include:

- People who use Facebook are more often less satisfied with the time and less satisfied with their lives.
- When other people are seen as happier or more successful in their social media posts,

people experience less self-esteem and more fear and jealousy.

- The increased use of smartphones at home is associated with greater conflict when working at home.
- More time in technology is associated with more combustion.
- The increased presence of technology in the bedroom is associated with lack of sleep.

This technology can be very addictive, making it easy to fall into models that are too often used. When you are with a loved one who is always on the phone, you know firsthand what the potential for technological breakthroughs is in relationships. But even if we find that constantly using other people is annoying, we can participate in the same behavior.

Take a few minutes to think about your own connection to your cellphone and other screens, and see how often you use your cellphone or tablet in the next few days. In another sense, while the whole world waits for us on our smartphone, the view never changes when we are stuck on the screen. Think about whether it might be a good idea to extend the time you spend in real life - for example:

- Activate the Do not disturb function if you want to take a short break from your phone.
- Sometimes leave your phone at home.

- Turn off notifications, so your phone doesn't encourage you to interact.
- Take your time to eat without technology.
- Make social media less accessible (for example, uninstall it from your smartphone).
- Minimize the number of applications you use, because each of them adds to the reasons that you will find on your cellphone.
- Exchange your smartphone for conventional phones. Although I know that this option sounds extreme, I feel it is liberating when I do it for three years.

Spend time outside

Being outside the home is good for our welfare. For example, living in a greener area is associated with better mental health. A study by Ian Alcock and his colleagues found that those who moved to greener areas had improved mental health later in life for a period of three years. Part of the positive impact of a greener environment seems to be due to the greater ability to walk in free time. Green spaces such as parks also function as meeting points for friends in the neighborhood and facilitate social connections.

It also seems to have the direct advantage of being in a natural, non-human environment. For example, we can enjoy the natural beauty around us while hiking in the forest and maybe even find a sense of spiritual connection. Weather in nature also gives us time not to deal with traffic, constant bombardment through advertising and entertainment, and automatic alert for potentially threatening people.

There is also evidence from laboratory studies that seeing natural scenes attack the parasympathetic nervous system and help restore it after stress. Related results show that walking in the natural environment (yard with trees scattered near the university where the study was conducted) compared to walking in urban areas caused a decline in Romania and reduced activity in the area. The brain region is related to Rome.

In short, there are enough reasons to spend time outdoors. Where can you spend more time experiencing the satisfaction and stress relief offered by nature?

SERVE OTHERS

Self-care is a selfish endeavor. The better we feel, the more we can give to others. The converse is also true: the more we do for others, the better we feel. In fact, research shows that helping others improve symptoms of anxiety and depression.

Why does it really help others to take care of themselves? Researchers in this field have offered several possible explanations:

1. Focusing on others can free us from our own suffering.
2. Helping others convey meaning and purpose.

3. Pro-social behavior can cause the release of oxytocin, which is involved in trust and attachment to others.
4. There is something inherent in doing good things for others that can stimulate the release of dopamine.
5. Reaching out to others can reduce activities in our stress response system.

There are many ways to serve others:

- Show support when someone we care about has a problem
- A loving reaction when someone makes a mistake
- Get friends for lunch
- Make our partner's day easier
- Be kind with other drivers
- Listen carefully to others
- Build others with our words
- Volunteers to help people in disadvantaged situations. We have to get out of the way to help someone who might never return the favor

We donate real objects; we don't need people to use them

- Helping neighbors with gardening
- Prepare food for someone in need

- Donate money to charities whose work makes sense to us
- Visit someone we know at the hospital

Helping others not only makes us happier but is also contagious. Behavior helps us to breed while others respond to benefits in the form of goods.

What choices can you use this week to brighten someone's day - and yourself? You can even get started right away.

Our minds are good at concentrating on what is wrong in our lives to exclude what is going well. However, if we can understand and appreciate the good things in our lives, we often find that we have more happiness than we might think.

Gratitude is associated with various positive aspects, including better moods, less risk of depression, less stress, greater life satisfaction, and stronger relationships. These effects can even be observed in simple short-term thanksgiving practices.

For example, the research team asked participants to write down things they were grateful for or some current problems in their lives; the gratitude exercise produces more positive emotions, a more positive outlook on life, and greater optimism for the future.

Gratitude also makes us more willing to help others, even at our own expense; when we find that our own resources are full, we tend to share them with others.

Our attention system is most sensitive to change,

and the things we have are constantly missing in the background of our lives. When we practice gratitude, we are often surprised at how grateful we should be. These may include:

- Your bed every night
- People in your life who care about you
- Clothing that covers your body
- A planet full of life
- Stars that warm your planet and allow photosynthesis
- Foods that nourish your body and nourish your efforts
- Electricity, running water and air conditioning
- Transportation
- A relatively safe environment
- Lungs that supply oxygen to every cell in your body and release carbon dioxide
- The brain that presents all your experiences
- The heart that pumps your blood
- Your five senses

And the list continues things we often don't pay attention to and appreciate until we realize that we can lose them. How many times have we noticed how nice it is to be healthy after an illness? We can even find things we are thankful for in our problems. For example, we might have difficulty bringing a child to the emergency room in the middle of the night, but we might be grateful that we have 24/7 access to medical care. A word of caution here - be careful when asking others to be grateful when they are having a hard time. He can easily feel illegitimate or refuse to struggle with what they are doing.

There are many ways to practice gratitude, such as:

- Write down the things you are thankful for each day (this bedtime activity can even improve your sleep)
- Take a few minutes to remember the things you are grateful for
- Say your thanks to someone in your life
- Send a letter to someone where you say thank you
- Practice gratitude meditation
- Recent research shows that thanking others is even more effective than just thinking about it - and is probably most effective when we are depressed. Take a moment to think about what you are grateful for in your life.

AFTERWORD

We always have potential friends with us - someone who will hopefully talk to us, praise our success, support us when we are down, plan a pleasant experience for us, give us the opportunity to use our strengths, and make ourselves friendly challenged. Unfortunately, we often play the role of our own enemies, hurrying to criticize and slowly forgive, protect ourselves from exercise, reduce sleep, eat junk food, and minimize our joie de vivre.

The practices that we see in this chapter will take you to a totally different approach: plan your life the way you want someone you love to have it. These packages take into account your basic nutritional needs, deep sleep, and constant exercise. This includes managing the inevitable stressors you encounter and spending time in nature. Finally, some of the sweetest things you can do for yourself are to express gratitude and give something to others.

These practices work well together. For example, research on the Mediterranean lifestyle not only shows nutritional benefits but also increases involvement in social and physical activities. One study found that the Mediterranean diet alone reduced the risk of depression by 20%, while more physical activity and more socialization led to a 50% reduction.

Ready to implement your plan? You can start with these steps. First, focus on what matters most to you:

1. Think about treating yourself as someone you care about. How do you want to be better?
2. Plan and start a consistent routine that prioritizes your sleep.
3. Make positive changes to your meal plan by, for example, preparing certain amounts of food at home each week.
4. Add more exercise to your day. Start slowly and wake up gradually.
5. Create a stress management plan. This includes small daily activities (e.g., relaxing music on the way home), larger weekly activities (e.g., yoga classes), and monthly activities (e.g., professional massage).
6. Spend more time in nature during your week: If possible, combine time outside the home with social contact.
7. Look for small ways to serve others every day, as well as larger aid projects that need to

be done routinely (e.g., weekly voluntary work at a food bank).

8. Write down three things for which you are grateful every night before going to sleep.

Panic attacks can be a terrible experience for anyone, but with the right tools and techniques, anyone can overcome them and live a full life.

The method described in this book will help you take responsibility again. So if you ever feel another attack, you will have everything you need to regain control quickly.

You now have a tool to reduce the frequency of attacks until only memory remains.

You can do it. That is not difficult. If you really want to change and eliminate a panic attack, you can achieve it using the steps outlined in this book.

Now go there and live your life according to your requirements!!!

Manufactured by Amazon.ca
Acheson, AB

10977340R00076